RESPONSIBILITY

RESPONSIBILITY

ITS DEVELOPMENT THROUGH
PUNISHMENT AND REWARD

BY

LAURENCE SEARS

SUBMITTED IN PARTIAL FULFILLMENT OF
THE REQUIREMENTS FOR THE DEGREE OF
DOCTOR OF PHILOSOPHY, IN THE FACULTY
OF PHILOSOPHY, COLUMBIA UNIVERSITY

NEW YORK   M·CM·XXXII

COLUMBIA UNIVERSITY PRESS

PRINTED IN THE UNITED STATES OF AMERICA
GEORGE BANTA PUBLISHING COMPANY, MENASHA, WISCONSIN

TO MY
MOTHER
AND
FATHER

PREFACE

A word of explanation is necessary as to the plan and purpose of this study. It is an analysis of those types of control or education which may be called moral as distinguished from legal or physical coercion, and which aim at the development of responsibility. It consists of three parts. There is first an analysis of this problem as made by certain ethical theorists. These seven men were chosen, both because of their intrinsic significance, and because of the influence they have had. In dealing with them there has been no attempt made at an exhaustive analysis. Nor, on the other hand, has the study been limited to a mere description of those aspects of their theories which bear only upon the immediate issue. In each case enough of the system has been given to make the particular question with which we are concerned emerge in its proper setting.

The second part is an abstract of twelve case histories of problem children. It was felt that any fruitful study of moral responsibility needs empirical evidence. For that reason a careful study was made of fifty elaborate histories of children ranging in age from about eight to about eighteen. A word may be necessary as to why children were selected rather than adults. The answer is simple: because it was possible to get very much more detailed and accurate studies of children than it was of adults. These particular cases are based on data recorded by experts in the field of clinical child guidance. It was access to this very carefully compiled mass of data which made possible the factual analysis required for this particular study. The only basis for selecting the cases was their completeness. It is to be regretted that it was not possible to include a complete record of all fifty cases. Since that was not feasible, twelve were chosen for special presentation because of their particular significance.

The third part is concerned with a reëxamination of the theories put forth in the first part in the light of the empirical data which emerged in the second part. The fundamental premise of this study is that no merely logical analysis of an ethical situation is adequate unless there is added to it an empirical examination of the facts, and a testing of the conclusions. It is by no means a new discovery that theory and practice have all-too-frequently been divorced; that those who have formulated the ethical theories of how society was to exercise control and those who have actually done this have not always walked hand in hand. Yet it would seem that such a uniting of forces would be useful to each group.

There is no thought that this is in any sense final. The conclusions are necessarily tentative, and are intended merely as a contribution to the vast amount of work that must be done if we are to have an experimentally verified ethics.

It is a pleasure to record my indebtedness: to Professor John J. Coss of Columbia University for his courtesy and generous encouragement, to Professor Herbert Schneider under whose guidance the work was carried out, and whose assistance was as helpful as his criticisms were pertinent, and to Professor John L. Childs of Teachers College, Co-

lumbia University, who for many years has given an intellectual stimulus which has been a delight and an inspira-
tion. I owe to Dr. Marion Kenworthy my initial interest in
this problem, and it was her skill and wisdom which showed
me new possibilities in the development of moral responsibility. To Elizabeth and Sidney Gamble goes my gratitude for
a friendship which has meant unfailing help and encouragement. Finally, I want to express my thanks to my wife for
her painstaking assistance and her rare insight without which
this book could not have been written.

I wish to acknowledge the courtesy of the Macmillan Company in permitting me to quote from *The Origin and Development of the Moral Ideas* by Westermarck, of Henry Holt
and Company in permitting me to quote from *Human Nature
and Conduct* by John Dewey, and the Stratford Company
in permitting me to quote from *The Story of Punishment*
by H. E. Barnes.

CONTENTS

Part One

A SURVEY OF THEORIES OF RESPONSIBILITY

Part Two

A STUDY OF THE DEVELOPMENT OF RESPONSIBILITY IN TWELVE CHILDREN

Part Three

AN EVALUATION OF ETHICAL THEORIES IN THE LIGHT OF THE EMPIRICAL DATA

PART ONE

A SURVEY OF THEORIES OF RESPONSIBILITY

Chapter I

UTILITARIANISM—PRAISE AND BLAME AS INSTRUMENTS FOR SOCIAL CONTROL

Jeremy Bentham (1748-1832)

In discussing the problem of moral responsibility, one finds a fresh point of departure in the work of Jeremy Bentham. He set all ethical problems in a new light; from his time on there was a leaven at work which made ethical speculation less tenuous and more fruitful.

He was reacting from authoritarianisms, from all ethical theories which had their basis in tradition rather than in a concrete examination of human capacities and needs. He sought an empirical basis for morals which would give something of the same assurance that the scientist was finding in his laboratory.

His major premise is well known: that men are moved ultimately by the desire for pleasure and the fear of pain; and that, therefore, happiness (the predominance of pleasure over pain) is the moral criterion.

Nature has placed mankind under the governance of two sovereign masters, pain and pleasure. It is for them alone to point out what we ought to do as well as to determine what we shall do. On the one hand the standard of right and wrong, on the other the chain of causes and effects, are fastened to their throne. They govern us in all we do, in all we say, in all we think: every effort we can make to throw off our subjection will serve but to demonstrate and confirm it.—*Principles of Morals and Legislation,* ch. i.

By the principle of utility is meant that principle which approves or disapproves of every action whatever according to the tendency it appears to have to augment or diminish the happiness of the party whose interests are in question.—*Ibid.,* ch. i.

The greatest happiness of all those whose interest is in question is the right and proper, and the only right and proper and universally desirable end of human action.—*Ibid.,* ch. i.

It is apparent that Bentham was strongly influenced by Hobbes' view that man in the state of nature is not as well off as he is in society, or to put it in Bentham's terms, it is only in society that there is any opportunity for man to achieve happiness. For this reason it is to man's advantage to give up certain of his personal desires since in the long run the gain in happiness would be greater than the loss. Bentham does not follow Hobbes in holding that the basis of society is some kind of social contract. Indeed, as will be shown later, he apparently believed that a man was privileged to reopen the question at any time as to whether or not it was to his advantage to obey the laws of the society in which he lived. And obversely society must see that it always is to his advantage to obey its dictates. For Bentham society is no metaphysical unit whose laws are to be equated with reason or even with any absolute justice, but simply a group which finds greater opportunity for happiness through coöperation than through anarchy, or individual isolation. For each individual there is a continual calculation as to the advantages accruing from obedience or disobedience. It is purely a matter of expediency, both for society and the individual.

It should be made clear, however, that Bentham saw in society more than merely a means to other ends. Indeed, the assumption that human nature takes pleasure in social actions is at the heart of his entire theory. Men seek their own happiness, but one of their most basic desires is for the satisfaction of the motive of benevolence:

It cannot but be admitted that the only interests which a man at all times and upon all occasions is sure to find adequate motives for consulting are his own. Notwithstanding this there are no occasions on which a man has not some motives for consulting the happiness of other men. In the first place, he has, on all occasions, the purely social motive of sympathy and benevolence; in the next place, he has, on most occasions, the semi-social motives of amity and love of reputation.—*Ibid.*, ch. xix.

It is important to realize how fundamental this was for the entire utilitarian position. By finding in human nature that which identified personal satisfaction with social good Bentham was able to meet one of the most difficult and persistent ethical problems that men had faced. It is not implied that this aspect of Bentham's theory was new. It was, in fact, the commonplace of 18th century, deistic moral theory. Bentham, however, did make it more explicit, and he gave it a more basic position in his system. To the query of why men should consider the interests of others as their own, many answers had come back. Some had said that it was the will of God; others that punishment would inevitably follow, either in this life or in the one to come, if the social duties were not fulfilled. Bentham replied that there need not be any such sharp dichotomy between a person's interests and his social responsibilities. He was not an impractical dreamer seeing an absolute conjunction of personal and social interests; he spent much of his life devising legislative codes which would help bring this about. But he did believe that human nature was such that it was necessary for the individual to find his greatest happiness in society.

To the theory of "natural rights" so prevalent in his day Bentham was an unwavering foe.

Rights are the fruits of the law, and of the law alone. There are no rights without law—no rights contrary to the law—no rights anterior to the law.—*Collected Works,* III, 221.

The only rights are those which it is expedient for society to grant, and correlatively there are no obligations save those which society can enforce. It was preëminently a practical theory of which even so consistent an opponent as T. H. Green could say: "no other theory has been available for the social and political reformer, combining so much truth with such ready applicability."

In dealing with the problem of rights and obligations one inevitably faces the question as to the utility of praise and blame. Bentham rarely deals with this issue specifically, and the reasons for this omission will be discussed later. But much light is thrown on the question by his treatment of allied issues, and by inference from his general position.

In considering the utility of praise and blame it is important to realize the different bases for their use. If we hold that there are observable laws of behavior, which have no inherent relationship with our own satisfactions, and which we violate through deliberate perversity, then blame is directed toward the sinner as being his due. Punishment is a justification of these laws of right and wrong, and any instrumental value is secondary. But it would seem that this position is hardly justifiable on the utilitarian basis either from the point of view of individual happiness or of social control. When as a psychological basis there is held the belief that all men are seeking pleasure or satisfaction, then a dissatisfaction can be used for purposes of control. Praise or blame are therefore relevant only to the satisfaction or dissatisfaction which others feel toward *his* satisfactions. Good is that which brings satisfaction, bad is that which does not. But what is good for one, may be bad for another, and vice versa.

From the social point of view utilitarianism does not eliminate praise and blame, but it does give them an entirely different status. They can no longer be directed against the individual for the pupose of arousing him to a sense of duty as opposed to the pursuit of happiness. If used at all, they must be either educational instruments for the instruction of the individual in this pursuit, or else means of insuring the greatest happiness of the greatest number.

Duty has an entirely different connotation, according to whether or not one accepts in the main Bentham's criterion. If satisfaction in one form or another, be it pleasure, happiness, or self-realization, is the goal of all human endeavor, the word "duty" has no individual meaning. "I ought" in any single individual's moral economy becomes synonymous with "I want," and duty is equated with desire intelligently pursued. But obligation and punishment have socially the function of forcing the individual to take account of the happiness of others as this is promoted by the laws of society, or of helping him to form habits which will aid him in discovering greater satisfactions by avoiding the consequences of causing pain to others.

When we turn to Bentham we find that he has largely carried out the implications of his position. In his analysis of what is meant by "disposition" he takes the position which we would expect:

A man is said to be of a mischievous disposition, when by the influence of no matter what motives, he is *presumed* to be more apt to engage, or form intentions of engaging, in acts which are *apparently* of a pernicious tendency than in such as are apparently of a beneficial tendency; of a meritorious or beneficent disposition in the opposite case.

It is evident that the nature of a man's disposition must depend upon the nature of the motives he is apt to be influenced by; in other words, upon the degree of his sensibility to the force of such and such motives. For his disposition is, as it were, the sum of his intentions. . . Now, intentions, like everything else, are produced by the things that are their causes; *and the causes of intentions are motives.* If, on any occasion, a man forms either a good or a bad intention, it must be by the influence of some motive.—P. of M. and L., ch. ii.

His position becomes clearer when we see what he means by motives.

If they (motives) are good or bad, it is only on account of their effects: good, on account of their tendency to produce pleasure, or avert pain; bad, on account of their tendency to produce pain, or avert pleasure. Now the case is, that from one and the same motive, and from every kind of motive, may proceed actions that are good, others that are bad, and others that are indifferent.

And again:

A motive is substantially nothing more than pleasure or pain operating in a certain manner. Now pleasure is in itself a good; nay, even setting aside immunity from pain, the only good. . .

It follows, therefore, immediately and incontestably that there is no such thing as any sort of motive that is in itself a bad one. If motives are good or bad, it is only on account of their effects.—P. of M. and L., ch. x.

In this categorical statement that motives are good or bad only in relation to their effects, he has formulated a practical criterion for estimating those which should be praised (i.e., give pleasure) and those which should be blamed (i.e., give pain).

When we turn to his treatment of praise and blame, we find him using the old terminology, "should" and "ought," but with a connotation which is in line with his general position.

The happiness of the individuals of whom a community is composed is . . . the sole standard, in conformity to which each individual *ought* to be made to fashion his behavior. But whether it be this, or anything else that is to be done, there is nothing by which a man can ultimately be *made* to do it, but either pain or pleasure.—P. of M. and L., ch. iv.

It would seem clear that while he means by duty that which society decides is necessary for the greatest happiness of the greatest number, there is no other means of inducing the individual to follow this "ought" than by inflicting pain or granting pleasure to him. Society can, therefore, see to it that its laws are so framed that duty and desire become synonymous, since it can make socially beneficial actions pleasurable and vice versa. It is important to note that when he refers to the will of society he seems to mean the will of the legislators, of elected representatives of society.

In *The Rationale of Reward,* Bentham deals with this question of the union of interest with duty.

The legislator should . . . endeavor to unite interest with duty.
. . But how is this union to be brought about?—what constitutes it? To create a duty and affix a punishment to the violation of it, is to unite a man's interest with his duty, and even
to unite it more strongly than by any prospect of reward. . .
In this phrase, by the word *interest, pleasure* or *profit* is understood: the idea designed to be expressed is, the existence of
such a provision in the law, as that conformity to it shall be
productive of certain benefits which will cease of themselves
as soon as the law ceases to be observed.—*Collected Works,*
II, 199.

It would perhaps make his position clearer if the various
steps in his argument were recapitulated. In the first place
there is his assumption that men seek pleasure. Added to
this is the belief that man is inherently social; that it is in
society that he reaches his greatest happiness. But it is obvious that not always does the individual's desire coincide
with the welfare of the greatest number. Because of this, society, through its legislators, has so to frame its laws that
duty and interest are synonymous. For Bentham the only
basis for duty is the will of the majority, expressed through
its legislators, as to what will make for the greatest happiness of the greatest number.

J. S. Mill commented on the fact that there is in Bentham's writings no reference to conscience, but it is apparent
that there is no need for it in his system. There is no duty or
obligation save that which society can enforce through its
rewards or punishments.

There follows as a logical corollary that men will continually be faced with the decision as to whether or not it is
to their interests to obey the laws, and their decision will be
the result, not of any adjustment of law to natural rights,

but of habit based on a calculation which each one makes for himself as to what he will gain or lose.

When faced with the question of how to make duty and interest coincide Bentham depended upon a series of rewards and punishments.

The business of government is to promote the happiness of society, by punishing and rewarding. . . In proportion as an act tends to disturb that happiness, in proportion as the tendency of it is pernicious, will be the demand it creates for punishment. —*Collected Works*, I, 70.

It is plain, therefore, that in the following cases punishment ought not to be inflicted.

1 Where it is groundless; where there is no mischief for it to prevent; the act not being mischievous on the whole.

2 Where it must be inefficacious; where it cannot act so as to prevent the mischief.

3 Where it is unprofitable, or too expensive; where the mischief it would produce would be greater than what it prevented.

4 Where it is needless; where the mischief may be prevented, or cease of itself, without it; that is, at a cheaper rate.— *Collected Works*, I, 178.

Elsewhere he states that rewards should be used in place of punishment when they do not cost more, but that on the whole it is more difficult to reward all those who do right than it is to punish those who disobey the laws.

His concern with the practical, legal aspects of moral issues is exemplified further in his analysis of real and apparent justice. He points out that there is in many cases a decided difference, and then goes on to say:

That a system of procedure be good—that it be well adapted to its proper end, it is not sufficient that the decisions rendered in virtue of it be conformable to real justice; it is necessary that they be conformable to apparent justice; to produce real justice, the only true way is to produce that which shall be in the eye of public opinion apparent justice. In point of utility, apparent justice is everything; real justice, abstracted from apparent justice, is a useless abstraction, not worth pursuing, and supposing it contrary to apparent justice, such as ought not to be pursued.

From apparent justice flow all the good effects of justice—from real justice, if different from apparent, none.—*Ibid.*, II, 21.

The preceding quotation would make clear, even without the many others which could be adduced, that Bentham was primarily interested in the legal and political aspect of punishment. But the question still remains as to how far he was interested in the individual who was punished. It may be granted that there is no hard and fast line to be drawn between the two problems. It is true, however, that the legislator's preoccupation with the greatest happiness of the greatest number blinds him to the happiness of any single individual.

Bentham was certainly not unconscious of this. In laying down his rules for punishment he insisted that it must reform the criminal in order that he may become happy, as well as deter others from committing a similar crime which interferes with the general happiness. He was intensely interested in Howard's plans for prison reform, and spent years of his life, besides a considerable amount of his own money, in endeavoring to convince the public of the value of what he called the Panopticon, a kind of penetentiary for the reform of criminals. Here they were to be taught to love work, and to be given at least an elementary education.

In the final analysis Bentham's theory as to the development of moral responsibility was very simple. Society must define individual responsibility in terms of the happiness of the entire group, and then develop it by rewarding those who accept their responsibility and punishing those who refuse to do so. What he lacked was the insight which modern psychology has brought into the complexity of our reactions. He assumed that since punishment brought unhappiness it would therefore bring about a reformation nearer to the will of society. He was forced later, however, to recognize the social utility of educational praise and blame, which, of course, greatly complicates the legal practice and theory with which he started. There is rarely any evidence of blame or punishment being regarded as the righteous expression of wrath at the violation of a duty; rather they are calculated instruments for the furtherance of the happiness of society.

Bentham is to be understood as one primarily interested in legal and social issues. That was his strength, for by keeping his eyes fixed on those problems he was able to devise the most practical rule that legislators had ever had. But it was also his weakness, in that he was not interested in analyzing the psychological factors which complicate legal systems. He did not try fundamentally to analyze why men do what is called wrong. He preferred to take them after they had been caught in the toils, and then try to reform them. He shared the general faith of his age in education, but he did not carry his inquiries far enough back. Had he done so there would have been a keener appreciation of the complexities of causal sequences which determine pleasure and pain. Perhaps that is only to say that Bentham was a child of the psychology of his time which was not yet interested in underlying causes and deep-hidden antecedents, but which constructed an over-simplified account of both happiness and reason in order to combat a hopelessly complicated and artificial society.

JOHN STUART MILL (1806-1873)

The utilitarian system of Jeremy Bentham had by no means gained universal acceptance by the middle of the 19th century, though James Mill had done much to popularize it. The intuitionist basis of morals still dominated. Ethical thought was controlled by the concepts of absolute rights and wrongs which could be known intuitively through conscience. Duty was therefore the obligation to follow what was known to be right, any failure to do so was sin, and blame and condemnation followed accordingly. Obviously those holding this view faced with alarm an ethical position which denied that there were any absolute rights, whose psychology declared that all men were seeking happiness, and for whom blame and punishment were only instruments for social control.

John Stuart Mill is to be understood as an apologist for utilitarianism who felt the need of demonstrating that the new theory incorporated all of the values of the old. He attempted to do this by employing the older terms such as conscience, duty, and obligation, but at the same time giving them new connotation. The result may have been to lessen men's fear of utilitarianism, but it did not make for clarity of expression. One misses the straightforward writing of Bentham, and the precision of Bain. Particularly in Mill's utilitarianism is it necessary to be continually on guard lest the use of old terminology betray one, and there are places where it seems that Mill, himself, has been so betrayed by the terms he was using.

He accepted Bentham's fundamental assumption that the search for pleasure and the avoidance of pain are the motivating forces of life.

The creed which accepts as the foundation of morals, Utility, or the Greatest Happiness Principle, holds that actions are right in proportion as they tend to promote happiness, wrong as they tend to produce the reverse of happiness. By happiness is intended pleasure, and the absence of pain; by unhappiness, pain, and the privation of pleasure.

And he adds

that pleasure, and freedom from pain, are the only things desirable as ends; and that all desirable things (which are as numerous in the utilitarian as in any other scheme) are desirable either for the pleasure inherent in themselves, or as means to the promotion of pleasure and the prevention of pain.— *Utilitarianism*, p. 6, "Everyman's Library."

Having accepted that principle, however, he qualifies it by answering one of the main criticisms which had been made. No sentence of Bentham's had been more often quoted than the one in which he insisted that pleasures could not be qualitatively compared, and said that push pin might be as good as poetry. This position Mill denies, though insisting that he is not affecting the general theory.

It is quite compatible with the principle of utility to recognize the fact, that some kinds of pleasure are more desirable and more valuable than others. It would be absurd that while, in estimating all other things, quality is considered as well as quantity, the estimation of pleasures should be supposed to depend on quantity alone.—*Utilitarianism*, p. 7.

This distinction, however, brings him at once up against the problem of how these qualities are to be judged. He holds that some are higher, more worth while, than others. But on what basis is this evaluation to be made? The intuitionists had a ready answer since they believed that there was inherent in man a faculty capable of immediately deciding, not only what was higher for them individually, but what was higher for all men. But Mill expressly disavows this solution, and proposes in its stead a solution similar to that of Aristotle. That pleasure is the more desirable which appeals to those competent to judge.

If I am asked, what I mean by differences of quality in pleasures, or what makes one pleasure more valuable than another, merely as a pleasure, except its being greater in amount, there is but one possible answer. Of two pleasures, if there be one to which all or almost all who have experience of both give a decided preference, irrespective of any feeling of moral obligation to prefer it, that is the more desirable pleasure.—*Ibid.*, p. 8.

This seems an amazing position for a utilitarian to take. One would think that inherent in a position which made the search for happiness central would be the belief that each man could best judge of that matter for himself. The intuitionist has another reason for judging; he wants to assess responsibility and blame, but this is legitimate and possible only if there is an infallible organ for moral judgment. Bentham would have admitted that it was necessary to evaluate which was better and which worse, but, and this is the important distinction, he would have done it purely for political and legal purposes. To be sure society must decide what makes for the greatest happiness of the greatest number, and the only way to do it is by counting votes. But Bentham would not have had the slightest interest in such an evaluation save for political expediency. Mill, however, seems to have been infected by the intuitionist's passion for moral judging, as is exemplified in another well-known passage:

It is indisputable that the being whose capacities of enjoyment are low, has the greatest chance of having them fully satisfied; and a highly endowed being will always feel that any happiness which he can look for, as the world is constituted, is imperfect. But he can learn to bear its imperfections, if they are at all bearable; and they will not make him envy the being who is indeed unconscious of the imperfections, but only because he feels not at all the good which those imperfections qualify. It is better to be a human being dissatisfied than a pig satisfied; better to be Socrates dissatisfied than a fool satisfied. And if the fool, or the pig, are of a different opinion, it is because they only know their own side of the question. The other party to the comparison knows both sides.—*Ibid.,* p. 9.

One is tempted simply to challenge the logic of the above passage. Granting for the moment the usefulness of making such a judgment there is still the problem of how it is to be made. Mill says that it is to be decided by those who have had an experience of both situations. But may one not question just how fully Mill was able to enter the life either of a pig or a fool, and whether after all he could evaluate their pleasures any more adequately than they could his? These are extreme cases; the problem is usually far more acute.

The utilitarian is on sure ground so long as he is evaluating for political purposes. By the same premise, it must be done in order to get norms for educating the child to take his place in society. It is thoroughly in line with utilitarian principles to stress as the goal the development of whatever inherent capacities the individual may have, feeling that in this way he will at once be the better member of society and the happier. But to try to say absolutely wherein happiness lies for each individual seems to go contrary to utilitarian logic. Here again, as we shall see, Mill's desire to make a utilitarian apologetic may have betrayed him into expressions which do not genuinely represent his beliefs.

Mill is in complete agreement with Bentham as to human nature being inherently social.

The social state is at once so natural, so necessary, and so habitual to man, that, except in some unusual circumstances or by an effort of voluntary abstraction, he never conceives himself otherwise than as a member of a body.—*Ibid.*, p. 29.

He also recognizes the place for legal rewards and punishments as a means of helping the individual find his satisfactions in ways which will lead to the welfare of society. In one respect he seems to have a more inclusive interest than did Bentham; Mill recognized the large place which education would have in any society organized on utilitarian principles.

As the means of making the nearest approach to this ideal, utility would enjoin, first, that laws and social arrangements should place the happiness, or (as speaking practically it may be called) the interest, of every individual, as nearly as possible in harmony with the interest of the whole; and secondly, that education and opinion, which have so vast a power over human character, should so use that power as to establish in the mind of every individual an indissoluble association between his own happiness and the good of the whole; especially between his own happiness and the practice of such mode of conduct, negative and positive, as regard for the universal happiness prescribes; so that not only he may be unable to conceive the possibility of happiness to himself, consistently with conduct opposed to the general good, but also that a direct impulse to promote the general good may be in every individual one of the habitual motives of action, and the sentiments connected therewith may fill a large and prominent place in every human being's sentient existence.—*Ibid.*, p. 16.

It is evident from the discussion of Bentham that on any strict utilitarian basis the word duty would have no real meaning, or would at least be equated with rational desire. So, too, with sacrifice. Logically speaking if all men are seeking satisfaction in some form or other, sacrifice is not only irrational, it is impossible. There might be the sacrifice of some immediate desire for the sake of a more distant one, but that could hardly be called sacrifice. Bentham had been forthright in his avowal of this position, but since his time criticism had been directed sharply against this aspect of his teaching. His psychology was considered to be oversimplified; Bain had already laid a sounder psychological foundation for understanding the motives of disinterestedness, and at times Mill seems to be aware of this.

In dealing with the concepts of right and wrong he refers to Bain, and says:

How we come by these ideals of deserving and not deserving punishment, will appear, perhaps, in the sequel; but I think there is no doubt that this distinction lies at the bottom of the notions of right and wrong; that we call any conduct wrong, or employ, instead, some other term of dislike or disparagement, according as we think that the person ought, or ought not, to be punished for it; and we say, it would be right to do so and so, or merely that it would be desirable or laudable, according as we would wish to see the person whom it concerns, compelled, or only persuaded and exhorted, to act in that manner.—*Ibid.*, p. 45.

In this passage he seems to treat moral obligation not as a transcendental fact, but as a problem in political economy, but another passage on the same page confuses the issue again.

We do not call anything wrong, unless we mean to imply that a person ought to be punished in some way or other for doing it; if not by law, by the opinion of his fellow creatures; if not by opinion, by the reproaches of his own conscience.

One is puzzled by the use of the word "conscience." Elsewhere Mill criticizes Bentham for not having made a place for conscience, but, as Leslie Stephens pointed out, there is no place for such a concept in a utilitarian ethic. A man may be coerced, or educated, so that he will find his satisfactions in such a way as not to interfere with the satisfactions of others. But if all men are controlled by a like motive, i.e., the search for pleasure, then they may mistake that which will bring pleasure, but they will hardly do that deliberately which will bring pain. And conscience, at least in its ordinary connotation, seems to involve deliberate imposition of non-pleasurable obligations. By the utilitarian premise conscience could mean no more than the awareness of social praise or condemnation.

Mill certainly accepts the pleasure-pain basis of Bentham.

It results from the preceding considerations, that there is in reality nothing desired but happiness. Whatever is desired otherwise than as a means to some end beyond itself, and ultimately to happiness, is desired as itself a part of happiness, and is not desired for itself until it has become so. Those who desire virtue for its own sake, desire it either because the consciousness of it is a pleasure, or because the consciousness of being without it is a pain, or for both reasons united; as in truth the pleasure and pain seldom exist separately, but almost always together, the same person feeling pleasure in the degree of virtue attained, and pain in not having attained more. If one of these gave him no pleasure, and the other no pain, he would not love or desire virtue, or would desire it only for the other benefits which it might produce to himself or to persons whom he cared for.—*Ibid.*, p. 35.

And yet in spite of this explicit statement we find him ranking sacrifice, which, as has been pointed out, on the utilitarian basis has, at least, an ambiguous place, as the highest virtue.

Though it is only in a very imperfect state of the world's arrangements that any one can best serve the happiness of others by the absolute sacrifice of his own, yet so long as the world is in that imperfect state, I fully acknowledge that the readiness to make such a sacrifice is the highest virtue which can be found in man.—*Ibid.*, p. 15.

In dealing with the question of duty he is equally ambiguous. It will be recalled that Bentham had bluntly used the term to denote those obligations which society could enforce, and that he held that there was every reason to expect that men would continually query whether or not it was to their advantage to obey the laws of society. There was no duty save that which, through a system of rewards and punishments, was to the individual's advantage to follow. That is very different from Mill's position:

I must repeat again, what the assailants of utilitarianism seldom have the justice to acknowledge, that the happiness which forms the utilitarian standard of what is right in conduct, is not the agent's own happiness, but that of all concerned. As between his own happiness and that of others, utilitarianism requires him to be as strictly impartial as a disinterested and benevolent spectator.—*Ibid.*, p. 16.

It is difficult to reconcile such a statement with belief "that there is in reality nothing desired but happiness," or that virtue is always desired because of the pleasure involved. If that is true then the statement that "utilitarianism requires him to be as strictly impartial as a . . . spectator" is without meaning.

One also wonders at the dichotomy which he makes between the individual's and society's welfare. Bentham would have said that naturally it is the agent's own happiness which is of concern to him, and that it is up to the legislators to see to it that his happiness coincides with the happiness of the greatest number. Not only does Mill's position make an impossible psychological demand according to utilitarianism, but it robs the theory of its value as an instrument of social control. As has been pointed out, Mill is apparently clear as to the psychological basis of duty, but he seems to want to keep its conventional status intact lest people be frightened at the loss of the old concepts.

When we turn to the question of the place of praise and blame in his thought we find little that is specific, and, as with Bentham, we must proceed largely by inference. Logically it would seem that they would have precisely the same place with him as with Bentham, i.e., as instruments of social control.

With his ambiguity, however, as to the basis for duty and obligation, it is difficult to be certain as to just what place he does give to praise and blame. We cannot be sure when he speaks of "actions which are blamable" whether he is using the terms in Bentham's sense or not. But it would seem, at times, at least, that by them he means more than just the fixed penalties of legal control.

It is interesting that, like Bentham, he feels the sentiment of vengeance to be natural.

The sentiment of justice, in that one of its elements which consists of the desire to punish, is thus, I conceive, the natural feeling of retaliation or vengeance, rendered by intellect and sympathy applicable to those injuries, that is, to those hurts, which wound us through, or in common with, society at large. This sentiment, in itself, has nothing moral in it; what is moral is, the exclusive subordination of it to the social sympathies, so as to wait on and obey their call.—*Ibid.*, p. 48.

Like Bentham, he does not at all critically evaluate how useful an instrument of social control vengeance is, but assumes that so long as it operates through sympathy it is valuable.

In the main Mill added little to what Bentham had said. One exception might be noted, i.e., his recognition that the development of character was more than just a legislative matter. He saw the inadequacy of the purely legal approach, and he thereby paved the way for the psychological contribution of Bain.

ALEXANDER BAIN (1818-1903)

The significance of Alexander Bain in the development of utilitarianism lay in his contribution to its psychological basis. As we have seen, Bentham based his theory on a definite psychology, but it was a very simple one. Bain, while accepting the main assumptions, differed at certain points, and also raised some issues of which Bentham was apparently unaware. The result was that in the work of Bain, utilitarianism reached its most instructive form.

Bentham's psychology seemed to make life essentially passive, awaiting sensations from without to move it. Therein he was only accepting the physics of his day which held that any body was in a state of rest unless moved by some external force. But this view had wide psychological implications. For Bentham pleasure and the desire to avoid pain were the forces which kept men active; once remove them and man would lapse back into impassivity.

Bain broke with this assumption. He held that life is basically active, and that it does not need external forces to move it. He held that movement is characteristic of the child from the beginning, only the movements are random, without direction. And feelings of pain and pleasure are not motivating but directional. If one of these random movements brings satisfaction there will be a tendency to repeat it; if it has brought pain there will be an aversion to it. Hence by his system the feelings of pain and pleasure occupy as large a place as they do with Bentham, but a different one.

Bain's next assumption is that these random movements according to the satisfaction involved become more or less solidified into habits, either positive or negative. And the important thing to realize is that these habits may persist long after the feeling basis has been forgotten. A child forms a particular way of reacting because of satisfactions involved. The situation changes, but that particular habitual way of acting remains though the child completely forgets why he started doing it.

This contribution of Bain to utilitarian theory was useful in many important ways: e.g., in what he has to say about sacrifice. Bentham had endeavored to explain it on the grounds of the benevolent instincts plus the desire for reward and the fear of punishment. But this did not seem to tell the entire story. There were plenty to insist that there

was a genuinely disinterested sacrifice where neither reward
nor punishment entered. And they pointed out that it seemed
a little paradoxical for a man to find such pleasure in benevolence that he sacrificed his life, and with it the hope of any
further satisfactions.

Bain fully recognizes the reality of sympathy and sacrifice.

There is a class of pleasures whose nature it is to take in other
sentient beings, as is implied in all the social affections. We
have further a tendency to enter into the pains of those about
us, to feel these as if they were our own, and to minister to
their relief exactly as we should treat our personal sufferings.
This power of sympathy is a fact in human nature of very
extensive operation, and is constantly modifying, and running
counter to, the selfish impulses properly so called. It is not true,
therefore, that men have always performed their duties only
so far as the narrow self was implied in them, although, of
course, these other impulses belonging to our constitution are
likewise our "self" in another acceptation.—*The Emotions and
the Will,* 3d ed., p. 267.

In trying to account for this behavior he is as strenuously
opposed to some innate moral sense dictating our duty as
was Bentham. He strongly denies that there is a certain
faculty in the human mind that enables us to define what is
right, and that dictates the times we should show sympathy
or sacrifice ourselves.

Bain explains sympathy in terms of what he calls a Fixed
Idea, or habit as we would say today.

I have always been disposed to regard sympathy as a remarkable and crowning instance of the Fixed Idea, which is to
make it an intellectual fact, or as much so as any fact conver-
sant with emotions can be. It has this in common with the
Fixed Idea, that it clashes with the regular outgoings of the
Will in favour of our pleasures. . . The ancient habit of

acting with others, the intense preconception of personality, would give an interest in everything relating to persons; there might not be a felt pleasure attending it on all occasions, there might be a good deal of the reverse; yet at one time or other, in the history of the sympathetic growth, there have been innumerable experiences of pleasure and relief from pain, which on the whole leave a cheering or exhilarating impression, and, irrespective of this, a strong habit of giving way to the expression of feeling in those about us. This habit once contracted, the effect will often arise without any conscious pleasure, or with the pleasure more than neutralized by the painful consequences of the sympathy.—*Ibid.*, p. 121.

In other words, at certain points in the individual's experience he has found so much satisfaction in the exercise of sympathy that that way of reacting becomes a habit. And, as Bain says, when that habit is once formed it will operate even though no conscious pleasure is expected, or even when the pleasure is outweighed by the pain involved. Sympathy and self-sacrifice then do not in their origins go beyond self interest, but they do operate as seemingly disinterested motives.

It is interesting to see the somewhat different attitude Bain has from Bentham as regards the social instincts. The latter based social reactions primarily on the benevolent instinct. Bain, in so far as he does make it instinctive, holds that it lies primarily in the physiological pleasures of touch and embrace; a curious prevision of certain of the behavioristic tenets.

It is apparent that social activity is for Bain by no means inevitable. It depends upon the reactions which a child associates with its early, perhaps random, experiments in sympathy and sacrifice. If they are satisfying, a habit will result which will operate through life. There is, thus, in his system a very large place given to education, and the deliberate forming of such attitudes in people. Included in this educational process would be the typical utilitarian view of the place of rewards and punishments. He thoroughly agrees with Bentham in believing that society should carefully enforce its will through making antisocial behavior unpleasant.

He makes an interesting reference in the first of the quotations given above to "the narrow self." He seems to have believed in the possibility of developing an inclusive, as opposed to a narrow, self; that the self might be so expanded that it takes in other persons. That would be a further basis for holding that there is no real sacrifice. In thus accounting for sympathy and sacrifice Bain met the most fundamental of the objections to utilitarianism, and none of the later exponents have materially added to his analysis.

He makes no marked contribution to what Bentham had said in regard to duty:

I may next remark upon the sense of duty in the Abstract under which a man performs all his recognized obligations, without referring to any one of the special motives adverted to. There may not be present to his mind either the fear of retribution, the respect to the authority commanding, affection or sympathy towards the persons or interests for whose sake the duty is imposed, his own advantage indirectly concerned, his religious feeling, his individual sentiments in accord with the spirit of the precept, the infection of example—or any other operating ingredient prompting to the action, or planting the sting for neglect. Just as in the love of money for its own sake, one may come to form a habit of acting in a particular way, although the special impulses that . . . were the original moving causes no longer recur to the mind. This does not prove that there exists a primitive sentiment of duty in the abstract, any more than the conduct of the miser proves that we are born with the love of gold in the abstract.—*Ibid.*, p. 290.

He speaks here not as a political theorist like Bentham concerned to deny some concept of obligation, but as a psychologist who cannot find any such faculty. He does recognize social duties, but he is very explicit in defining what he means by them:

I consider that the proper meaning, or import, of these terms (Morality, Duty, Obligation, or Right) refers to the class of actions enforced by the sanction of *punishment*.

He is consistent in his attitude toward conscience.

Conscience . . . is an ideal resemblance of public authority, growing up in the individual mind, and working to the same end.—*Ibid.*, p. 264.

The first lesson that a child learns as a moral agent is obedience, or acting according to the will of some other person. There can be nothing innate in the notion thus acquired of command and authority, inasmuch as it implies experience of a situation with other human beings. The child's susceptibility to pleasure and pain is made use of to bring about this obedience, and a mental association is rapidly formed between disobedience and apprehended pain, more or less magnified by fear. The peculiarity attending the kind of evil inflicted, as a deterring instrument, is the indefinite continuance, or it may be, increase of the infliction until the end is secured. The knowledge of this leaves on the mind a certain dread and awful impression, as connected with forbidden actions; which is conscience in its earliest germ, or manifestation.—*Ibid.*, p. 285.

There is one passage which, though long, is so illuminating that it deserves to be quoted in its entirety. It might serve as an epitome of Bain's attitude toward the development of moral responsibility. It is at the close of his treatment of the will:

It not uncommonly happens that a delinquent pleads his moral weakness in justification of his offense. The school boy, on being found guilty of a breach of discipline, will sometimes defend himself by saying that he was carried away and could not restrain himself. In other words, he makes out a case closely allied to physical compulsion. He is frequently answered by the assertion that he could have restrained himself if he had chosen, willed, or sufficiently wished to do so. Such an answer is really a puzzle or paradox, and must mean something very different from what is apparently expressed. The fact is, the offender was in a state of mind such that his conduct followed according to the uniformity of his being, and, if the antecedents were exactly repeated, the same consequent would certainly be reproduced. In that view, therefore, the foregoing answer is irrelevant, not to say nonsensical. The proper form and the practical meaning to be conveyed is this, "It is true that, as your feelings then stood, your conduct resulted as it did; but I am now to deal with you in such a way, that, when the situation recurs, new feelings and motives will be present, sufficient, I hope, to issue differently. I now punish you, or threaten you, or admonish you, in order that an antecedent motive may enter into your mind, as a counteractive to your animal spirits or temper on another occasion, seeing that, acting as you did, you were plainly in want of such a motive. I am determined that your conduct shall be reformed, and therefore every time that you make such a lapse, I will supply more and stronger incentives in favour of what is your duty." Such is the plain unvarnished account of what the master intends in the address to his erring pupil. Though he may not state it so, he acts precisely in the spirit of the language I have now supplied. Finding a delinquency, he assumes at once that a repetition will occur if the same feelings and ideas arise under the same outward circumstances; and, accordingly, there is nothing left for him but to vary the antecedents, and make sure that a new and potent spur shall be mixed up with the previous combination, so as to turn the conduct in the direction sought.—*Ibid.*, p. 477.

As one analyzes this passage it is not difficult to find in it the essence, not only of Bain's theory of moral control, but of the utilitarians in general.

In the first place it is very clear that he has a genuine, deep interest in social control. There is no apparent desire to justify abstract justice or to vindicate a moral principle. But there is a decided enthusiasm for so adjusting individuals to their environment that society may function harmoniously.

On Bentham's assumption that men actually seek happiness or satisfaction, it was comparatively simple for society so to adjust rewards and punishments as to equate social welfare with personal happiness. Or, as Bain says in the above passage, he would: "supply more and stronger incentives in favour of what is your duty." There is a belief that the individual is not to be blamed since his action was inevitable. He is not to be regarded as a sinner to be shamed, but as a poorly educated person who needs new incentives to form more social habits.

While this view was a decided advance over previous theories it was obviously inadequate. On the basis of Bain's psychology, the process is now seen to be much more intricate than he realized. It is interesting to see how control had been shifted from the simple program of rewards and punishments for adults which Bentham advocated to Bain's emphasis on child education. The latter, however, had little understanding of the effect of the environment and the way control could be had through its manipulation. It remained for later investigators to stress this aspect.

Punishment is still for Bain the primary instrument of control, and fear of it helps form the habits of altruism and duty. The structure is at least partially empirical, open to frank examination. Since there are no antecedent principles to be upheld, each attitude and belief is to be measured by its social utility.

It is this empirical quality which encourages us to evaluate critically this theory. Was it sufficiently empirical? We can see issues that were not apparent then. Bain assumed that punishment worked. We now know more of the complexity of our reactions, and realize that we must carefully study the individual to see what kinds of punishment work, and what kinds do not. The same holds true of praise and encouragement.

Chapter II

EVOLUTION—PRAISE AND BLAME
GENETICALLY JUSTIFIED

Edward A. Westermarck (1862-   )

The ethical theories of Westermarck represent an approach almost completely divergent from those of Bentham, Mill, or Bain. Whereas these writers are moral in their approach, concerned primarily with social results, Westermarck is biological, concerned with the origin of moral emotions. The utilitarians were reformers; he was only incidentally concerned with this. They were primarily legal and political theorists; he scarcely mentions this aspect of morals.

That he recognizes the essential contradiction between his view and theirs is clear, since he brings out his fundamental belief through an examination of utilitarianism.

That the moral concepts are ultimately based on emotions either of indignation or approval is a fact. . . The moral concepts are essentially generalizations of tendencies in certain phenomena to call forth moral emotions. Very commonly, in the definition of the goodness or badness of acts, reference is made, not to their tendencies to evoke emotions of approval or indignation, but to the causes of these tendencies, that is, to those qualities in the acts which call for moral emotions. Thus, because good acts generally produce pleasure and bad acts pain, goodness and badness have been identified with the tendencies of acts to produce pleasure or pain.—*The Origin and Development of the Moral Ideas,* ch. i.*

* This quotation and the others from Westermarck, *The Origin and Development of the Moral Ideas,* are by permission of the Macmillan Company, publishers.

The opening sentence of the above quotation gives the clue to his entire view; moral concepts are based on emotions either of indignation or approval. The moral emotions for him do not result from any desire for control, but are thoroughly instinctive, being rooted ultimately in a desire for punishment, or the retributive emotions, as he calls them. He analyzes these retributive emotions into resentment on the one hand, and retributive kindly emotion on the other. Resentment, in turn, vents itself either in anger and revenge, or else in moral disapproval, while retributive kindly emotion works itself out as moral approval or else as non-moral retributive kindly emotions. It is the moral disapproval and moral approval which he calls the moral emotions.

It is worth noting that he apparently accepts a psychology which holds to instincts, so that having located the retributive emotions on an instinctive basis there is little that can be done save to direct them. This is the fundamental moral problem; to see that resentment goes toward moral disapproval and not toward revenge. The latter motive he regards as fundamentally immoral, but since there is an instinctive demand for some outlet for the retributive emotions it is found in moral disapproval and punishment.

He objects to the assumption that such a moral emotion has any character of universality or objectivity. He finds that this assumption of objectivity is due to the fact that in early society there was practically no difference of opinion, and also to the authority which is ascribed to moral rules. This being the case:

There can be no moral truth in the sense in which this term is generally understood. The ultimate reason for this is, that the moral concepts are based upon emotions, and that the contents of an emotion fall entirely outside the category of truth.

This does not imply, however, that there can be no science of ethics for:

It may be true or not that we have a certain emotion, it may be true or not that a given mode of conduct has a tendency to evoke in us moral indignation or moral approval. Hence a moral judgment is true or false according as its subject has or has not that tendency which the predicate attributes to it. If I say that it is wrong to resist evil, and yet resistance to evil has no tendency to call forth in me an emotion of moral disapproval, then my judgment is false. If the word "Ethics" then, is to be used as the name for a science, the object of that science can only be to study the moral consciousness as a fact.—*Ibid.*, ch. i.

This passage states the ethical problem as he sees it. He is concerned first with a fact; does some situation call forth a retributive emotion? If it does not, then there is no ethical question involved. If it does, then there is another problem to be considered, i.e., the channel this emotion shall take.

The rule of retaliation and the rule of forgiveness . . . are not so radically opposed to each other as they appear to be. What the latter condemns is, in reality, not every kind of resentment, but non-moral resentment; not impartial indignation, but personal hatred. It prohibits revenge but not punishment.—*Ibid.*, ch. iii.

His position is brought out clearly by his attitude toward punishment. He admits that there may be something in the view of punishment for purposes of social control, but he adds:

Punishment can hardly be guided exclusively by utilitarian considerations, but requires the sanction of the retributive emotion of moral disapproval.

It is a far call from utilitarianism to a position which holds that:

. . . punishment in the ordinary sense of the word always involves an express intention to inflict pain, whatever be the object for which pain is inflicted. We do not punish an ill-natured dog when we tie him up so as to prevent him from doing harm.

According to the principle of determent, the infliction of suffering in consequence of an offense is justified as a means of increasing public safety. The offender is sacrificed for the common weal. But why the offender only? It is quite probable that a more effective way of deterring from crime would be to punish his children as well.

Again, if punishment were to be regulated by the principle of reforming the criminal, the result would in some cases be very astonishing. There is no more incorrigible set of offenders than habitual vagrants and drunkards, whereas experience has shown that the most easily reformed of all offenders is often some person who has committed a serious crime. *Ibid., ch. iii.*

Is moral resentment directed toward the safety of society or the reformation of the criminal? Only incidentally. It

first of all . . . wants to raise a protest against wrong. And the immediate aim of punishment has always been to give expression to the righteous indignation of the society which inflicts it.

Nor is this a mere indulgence; it marks the very essence of right and wrong.

Since the remotest ages the aggressive attitude . . . has been connected with an instinctive desire to produce counter pain . . . we can hardly help being indulgent to the gratification of a human instinct which seems to be well-nigh ineradicable. It is this instinctive desire to inflict counter-pain that gives to moral indignation its most important characteristic. Without it, moral condemnation and the ideas of right and wrong would never have come into existence. Without it, we would no more condemn a bad man than a poisonous plant.—*Ibid.*, ch. iii.

Perhaps his position will be clarified if we remember what the underlying psychological assumption is of the utilitarians, i.e., that all men are seeking happiness. On such a basis, while society may condemn an act as interfering with the happiness of others, it can hardly look on the individual as being deliberately perverse, since he is only after the same thing as are all men. And it becomes the task of society so to reward or punish that the individual will consider others. Westermarck does not accept this assumption and so the person, himself, is regarded as willfully doing wrong. His "will" is wrong. He recognizes that unless the individual is regarded as deliberately harming another, it would be impossible to have the retributive emotion.

Let us once more remember that even a dog distinguishes between being stumbled over and being kicked; and this can neither be the result of discipline, nor have anything to do with the feeling of self-regarding pride. The reason is that the dog scents an enemy in the person who kicks him, but not in the one who stumbles.
We can hardly feel disposed to resent injuries inflicted upon us by animals, little children or madmen, when we recognize their inability to judge of the nature of their acts. They are not the real causes of the mischief resulting from their deeds, since they neither intended nor foresaw nor could have forseen it.—*Ibid.*, ch. xiii.

Without this assumption of deliberate perversity his entire structure would collapse.

Deliberate resentment considers the motives of acts.

Moreover, our anger abates, or ceases altogether, if we find that he who injured us acted under compulsion, or under the influence of a non-volitional impulse, too strong for any ordinary man to resist.

He frankly states that we must regard a man: "as existing independently of that which influences him." There is, thus, a will which is uncaused, standing aside to judge impartially as to what is right.

He cannot accept a belief that there are adequate causes for every act, for were that so there could be no moral emotion. Holding such a view it is obvious that praise and blame are not primarily instrumental; are not subject to any examination as to their usefulness. They are, rather, expressions of man's independent will, of righteous indignation or of moral approval.

One inevitably recurs to the question as to what is the basis for men's motives. Westermarck has ruled out the search for happiness. It can hardly be the obedience to duty since he repudiates a belief in any objective standard. Nor can it be self-expression since happiness would have to be admitted, if not as the goal, at least as the norm whereby success is to be measured. We can only say that Westermarck leaves the problem unsolved, unless "instinct" is a solution.

There are in his theory two fundamental psychological issues, which are complementary to each other. Are the feelings of indignation as natural as he assumes, and is there some part of the personality which is not motivated? Westermarck, himself, links the two issues together, but he does not make it clear whether the first follows because the second is assumed, or vice versa. In either case, he refuses to search for fundamental causes. And it is with this that we are most concerned. For with the development of clinical psychology we are beginning to see that a chain of causes does lie behind every act of vindictiveness, which explains it better than the supposed instinct does; and we are also realizing that we can get control to the extent that we can locate these specific underlying causes. Westermarck proves an excellent illustration of the fact that the emotion of blame and the search for causes are antithetical, a fact which he would be the first to admit.

Another issue which Westermarck entirely fails to investigate is the psychological result on the individual who is the recipient of these retributive emotions. To what extent are guilt feelings and other "moral" emotions destructive?

Because of his belief in retributive instincts he can see nothing that can be done save to direct the emotions of disapproval away from physical revenge into more constructive channels. He feels that this can be done, and that these moral emotions of approval and disapproval are the primary instruments of such control as is possible, *and therefore constitute a solution, rather than a problem.*

There is, hence, no critical examination as to how much they bring the desired results, nor, indeed, is he much interested in the question. His primary concern is to demonstrate the reality of these emotions, and then to prove that the "moral" channels are less destructive than the original, non-moralized forms of vengeance.

Westermarck is to be understood as one who found in the evolutionary method a new form of apologetics. He was primarily concerned with justifying conscience by discovering the origins of our beliefs and attitudes. It was here that he made his great contribution. As a statement of the fact that men have had strong emotions of indignation and approval, and as a description of the circumstances under which these emotions have become moralized, there can be little objection. It is, however, with his tacit assumption that they have been genetically explained when they are attributed to instincts that we are in disagreement. More recent psychology tends to point out that even patterns whose origins are buried in the dim past may change in a new environment, and that our instincts are by no means as rigid as was formerly supposed. The fact that men have reacted in specific fashions for untold eras is not final proof that they need to do so in the future.

CHAPTER III

IDEALISM—FINAL JUDGMENTS AND
MORAL RESPONSIBILITY

T. H. GREEN (1836-1882)

Fundamental in any ethical system is its interpretation of the self, and there could be no clearer illustration of this than the contrast between British idealism and utilitarianism. For their wide divergence begins at this point.

The utilitarians started with a group of discrete selves, each sharply separated from the other. No one can deny that such a view does represent an aspect of truth. Selves are more or less distinct, and no metaphysical subtleties can convince the majority of mankind to the contrary. Starting with this aspect of the self, however, there arises the problem of understanding man in his social relationships. The utilitarians answered it by pointing to the fact that one of the ways we get our pleasure is through our social contacts, that man is naturally altruistic.

The idealists have never been satisfied with this approach. Representative of their view are T. H. Green and F. H. Bradley. Green sees the self in an entirely different light than do the utilitarians. Not only, according to him, are selves not sharply differentiated, but ultimately they are only vehicles for a single, universal Self.

The very consciousness, which holds together successive events as equally present, has itself apparently a history in time. It seems to vary from moment to moment. It apprehends processes of becoming in a manner which implies that past stages of the becoming are present to it as known facts; yet is it not itself coming to be what it has not been?

It will be found, we believe, that this apparent state of the case can only be explained by supposing that in the growth of our experience, in the process of our learning to know the world, an animal organism, which has its history in time, gradually becomes the vehicle of an eternally complete consciousness. What we call our mental history is not a history of this consciousness, which in itself can have no history, but a history of the process by which the animal organism becomes its vehicle. "Our consciousness" may mean either of two things; either a function of the animal organism, which is being made, gradually and with interruptions, a vehicle of the eternal consciousness; or that eternal consciousness itself, as making the animal organism its vehicle and subject to certain limitations in so doing, but retaining its essential characteristic as independent of time, as the determinant of becoming, which has not and does not itself become. The consciousness which varies from moment to moment, which is in succession, and of which each successive state depends on a series of "external and internal" events, is consciousness in the former sense. It consists in what may properly be called phenomena; in successive modifications of the animal organism, which would not, it is true, be what they are, if they were not media for the realization of an eternal consciousness, but which are not this consciousness. On the other hand, it is this latter consciousness, as so far realized in or communicated to us through modification of the animal organism, that constitutes our knowledge, into which time does not enter, which are not in becoming, but are once for all what they are.—*Prolegomena to Ethics,* ed. of 1883, p. 72.

Each individual, then is to be understood only as an aspect of an inclusive Self. The goal for each is not greater individualization, but a deeper realization of this universal, social nature.

Holding such a definition of the self and its goal, Green
has an entirely different attitude as regards the place of
feeling. Most of the utilitarians had made feelings of happiness or pleasure the goal of life, and all of them had found
such feelings the norms for conduct. Green breaks with all
this.

The highest moral goodness is an attribute of character, in so
far as it issues in acts done for the sake of their goodness, not
for the sake of any pleasure or any satisfaction of desire.—
Principles of Political Obligation.

Green does not admit that feelings are either the goal or
the norm. Nor does he accept the position that we can directly and intuitively know the good. His solution is that of
Kant: that through reason and the dialectical method it is
possible to discover the laws of morality as surely as one
can discover the laws of motion. Through this method we
can discover intrinsically good acts, without regard to their
consequences.

The charge may be brought against the view of Green that
it did not regard the individual as an end. His desires and
pleasures had to be subordinated to a deeper purpose; his
character must be developed, not in the light of the search
for the greatest amount of happiness, but for the sake of
realizing his own universal Self. Green partly gets around
this difficulty by his use of the word "satisfaction." Strictly
speaking, in his system it should mean nothing more than as
if we said that a given quantity satisfied an equation. Actually as Green uses the term it seems at times to include
some feeling content; at least the use of the word prevents
one from seeing easily the full logic of his position.

It is important to see that control has been shifted from the external basis of the utilitarians to an internal position. For the utilitarians control was to be found through a system of rewards and punishments which would operate externally on the individual. For Green, since this is the most that society can do, its control is negative, to remove the obstacles which prevent the individual from realizing his highest self and character.

Green's view of duty was far from that of the utilitarians. Bentham had been perfectly explicit in saying that duty simply meant those requirements which society enforced, and that if a man did not find satisfaction in social behavior, duty in the sense of some abstract "ought" had no meaning. Duty for him had thus no meaning apart from legal obligation. Green, however, explicitly distinguished moral duty from legal obligation. In so doing he was not using the term in the Kantian sense, for he recognized that duty for Kant had largely been left empty, and therefore subject to caprice and tradition. Green was decidedly influenced by Hegel in making duty synonymous with the realization in the individual of the universal Self. Obviously this had wider implications than just the legal aspect would give.

The utilitarian would perhaps have had no quarrel with such a theory of self-realization so long as it was recognized that it was pursued because of the pleasure involved. But neither Hegel nor Green would admit that this pleasure was relevant. It has been pointed out that there was a certain ambiguity in Green's use of the word satisfaction, but it is clear that he believed that a man should seek this highest realization, not because of any feelings involved, but because he "ought" to see his responsibility to do so. Duty had, thus, a definite content for both Hegel and Green, but it was apart from any pleasure involved.

This position becomes clearer when we see what their view of punishment was. Hegel's attitude was that punishment was not founded on the needs of social safety but on a necessary logic of freedom. The criminal has a *right* to punishment since only in that way does society treat him as a rational being who acknowledges the rights of others as being implicit in the freedom he demands for himself. If he is punished in order to reform him, or for the purpose of influencing others, he is not being treated as a responsible agent.

Green, however, does not regard this position as being completely contrary to the utilitarian position. He recognizes that punishment may legitimately be preventative and reformatory, but its final function is, none-the-less, to bring the individual to a greater degree of self-consciousness.

His attitude is that punishment is not directed toward the moral guilt of the wrongdoer, nor for the purpose of reforming him. We cannot penetrate the will to discover its secrets, and, therefore, we cannot grade punishment according to degrees of guilt. On the other hand, if punishment were for the purpose of reformation it would deprive the criminal of the possibility of regenerating his own will. The function of punishment is to maintain proper *external* conditions, and not to deal with the inner will.

Here again ones sees clearly how control has been shifted from an external to an internal basis. Punishment cannot reform the will; it can only make possible the criminal's reformation of his own will by turning his attention to a higher, inner sanction. Punishment is a removal of obstacles.

Before an evaluation of this position as a basis for the development of responsibility can be made, it is necessary to see what its underlying premises are. It is obviously deeply concerned with the ultimate ends of life. Life is only to be understood in religious terms; in the light of the total process of which this present existence is only a part. This belief gives the self what is essentially a theological function. The political organization is simply concerned with the external conditions for this universal social life; it is most deeply concerned with the conditions which will permit of the progressive identification of the individual with the universal Self.

Another premise involved in Green's position is that "the agent is not a natural agent." In other words, the self is not a cause but an end. Since it is not a part of the natural order it is not subject to any law of cause and effect. Green does not argue for an indeterminist view. He accepts the fact that conduct is the result of the appeal of motives to the self. But he insists that this is moral freedom as well as determinism. He seems to be thinking of moral causation in terms of an Aristotelian final cause. And in this way the self is free in so far as it is conscious of its ends.

Green's theory of moral control may be summed up in a single phrase: "Moral control is self control." The only genuine control is that which the individual exercises over himself. Society can do some things. It can remove obstacles that lie in the way of an individual gaining control over himself. Practically speaking, this did bring Green fairly near the utilitarians, and he was very much alive to the social and political issues of his day.

Society can, also, give a man punishment as that which is rightfully due him. Punishment is not the infliction of an unpleasant experience either as a justification of a moral law, or, in utilitarian terms, as a means of bringing the individual into line with the will of a majority. It is rather a recognition of the dignity and worth of a human being. A man does wrong: were he not punished, there would be a tacit recognition that he was not responsible. That would be a supreme insult. Punishment, paradoxically, is society's tribute to the fact that he is a free, moral agent. If the individual persists in wrongdoing even after society has removed any obstacles, then judgment must fall.

How adequate a basis for control does this give? There is the same problem that is always faced when, through a desire to maintain some theory of human responsibility, the self is placed outside the chain of causal sequence. When that happens it becomes not only unpredictable but uncontrollable. The question of *why* an individual does wrong seems irrelevant. The *fact that* he does it entitles him to punishment. Because punishment is not instrumental there is little interest in searching for the causes that lie behind behavior, and make control possible.

As Dr. Dewey has pointed out, an attitude such as Green's tends to put the stress on the subjective motives and dispositions. "Meaning well" becomes the supreme value, and the result makes for a futile sentimentality rather than a genuine efficient means of control.

Green makes much of what may be called the *ideal* self, the self which acknowledges responsibility and accepts the implications of its freedom. The issue remains, however, as to whether this ideal self is a given datum, requiring only a setting where obstacles have been removed, or whether the *actual* self is only potentially responsible, needing persistent attention to causal sequences in order that through this social control it may be brought to its ideal fulfillment.

F. H. BRADLEY (1846-1924)

Bradley starts his *Ethical Studies* with a statement of the problem which is to concern him throughout the book; what do we mean by responsibility? The very question marks the wide divergence between himself and the utilitarians. They would hardly have been interested in it except in its social implications. The problem for them was the achievement of a technique for social control. With this initial difference it is inevitable that the ultimate conclusions should be very far apart.

Bradley plunges at once into the determinist controversy. In unmistakable terms he disavows any belief in freedom as it is usually defined.

. . . freedom in the usual sense means chance; you are free because there is no reason which will account for your particular acts, because no one, not even yourself, can possibly say what you will or will not, do next. You are accountable, in short, because you are a wholly unaccountable creature.—*Ethical Studies*, ch. i.

On the other hand, he strenuously refuses to admit that determinism does not permit of freedom, that it removes human responsibility. His proof of this is an appeal to common opinion.

The strongest proof that no connection whatever exists between belief in accountability and the mere idea of knowledge beforehand, is the fact that, for the faults we were sure beforehand we should commit, and which we know for certain we should commit again, we never for one moment doubt we are responsible.—*Ibid.*, ch. i.

Implicit in this position is a particular definition of the self, and, if it is possible to reduce Bradley's views to consistency it must be done through a study of this concept. In the first place he insists that a man's "habituated self does not cover his whole nature." This is, of course, a decided break from the psychology of Bain who would have denied that there could be any part of the personality which was not controlled by habit, and would have said, to use Bradley's own words, that this "means chance," and would result in a "wholly unaccountable creature."

Bradley gets around this dilemma by making a sharp distinction between the self and the character. The latter is derived and determined; the result of education and environment. The former is original, and stands above the empirical world. It is important to note that the self and the will are identical. This self or will is determined only by final causes, and he seems to feel that this means that human freedom and responsibility are preserved. But this raises one of the more fundamental issues. Throughout he seems to imply that a material or efficient cause is more determinative than a final cause, and, since it is only this latter cause which operates on the self, that it is more free than the character, which responds to the other types of causes. But are *final* causes any less *causes?*

Since the self is not determined, it is impossible to predict what it will do. There is no basis for judgment. Previous experience may give some hint, and previous attitudes may throw some light, but it is ultimately unpredictable. He goes farther; any attempt to understand this self is a violation of it. "To explain the origin of a man is utterly to annihilate him," and by "man" he means the self; this mysteriously motivated, but uncaused will.

In trying to see the values which he wishes to save, we find that he is afraid lest the element of self-sameness be lost by the determinists:

In reading our determinists, the one chance of their term bringing anything at all before the intellect, is for us to keep in sight a thing called a will, pushed and pulled by things called motives. Not only in the act of "I will" does Determinism entirely lose sight of the "I," and hence fail to recognize the characteristic of the will; not only does it hold by a will that *wills* nothing . . . but also, it ignores or denies the identity of the self in all the acts of the self, and without selfsameness we saw there was no possibility of imputation.—*Ibid.*, ch. i.

When one analyzes his viewpoint on this, as well as various other aspects of his philosophy, ultimately one finds this touchstone by which an ethical theory is judged true or false. Does it make room for judging, for imputation, for holding the individual responsible?

Granting the element of sameness in the self, then freedom is not to be regarded as an original part of the self, but as something to be achieved. "The man is free who realizes his true self." Freedom and determinism meet at this point. The man is free who is not controlled by his feelings, but who is motivated by the desire for self-realization. Apparently Bradley is laboring with the utilitarian assumption that motives are *internal* to the self. Admitting this, he is forced to find an *objective* final cause.

We cannot accept the theory that the end or motive is always the idea of a pleasure (or pain) of our own, which is associated with the object presented, and which is that in the object which moves us; but, though we do not admit that the motive is always, or in most cases, the idea of a state of our feeling self, yet we think it is clear that nothing moves unless it be desired, and that what is desired is ourselves. For all objects or ends have been associated with our satisfaction, (more correctly) have been felt in and as ourselves, or we have felt ourselves therein; and the only reason why they move us now is that, when they are presented to our minds as motives, we do now feel ourselves asserted or affirmed in them.—*Ibid.*, ch. ii.

The question which immediately presents itself is as to the reason why one should "desire" this self-realization. At times he identifies this desire with the feeling of satisfaction, but then he repudiates this explanation, and we are forced to realize that here, too, we are faced with an essentially mysterious will or self.

His attitude toward pleasure is ambiguous. At times he accepts happiness as an end, but rejects pleasure; at other times he seems to accept pleasure also as "the felt assertion of the will or self." And he goes on to say:

It is good because it accompanies and makes a whole with good activity, because it goes with that self-realization which is good; or secondly, because it heightens the general assertion of self, which is the condition of realizing the good in self.—*Ibid.*, Note to "Essay" 3.

It is difficult to reconcile these conflicting statements, but he is apparently arguing for the position that has always been popular; that happiness is a by-product, to be pursued indirectly.

If you want to be happy in the sense of pleased, you must not think of pleasure, but, taking up some accredited form of living, must make that your end, and in that case with moderate good fortune, you will be happy.—*Ibid.*, ch. iii.

There seem to be two reasons why Bradley has such difficulty in facing the feeling aspect of morals. In the first place he has an absolute disjunction between means and ends.

Pleasure is still ostensibly the end; but really it has ceased to be so, and, whether we know it or not, our way of living is an end to our minds, and not a mere means.—*Ibid.*, p. 91.

He sees the obvious fact that certain things are ends, are good in and for themselves. Therefore he makes the dialectical leap that they cannot, then, be means. If he were willing to admit that a thing can be both a means and an end he would not have the same problem. He could admit pleasure as an end and as a means; he could see that a specific good may be valuable both in itself and also for the pleasure it leads to.

The second reason lies in the fact that he feels that satisfaction may be a concomitant of a specific object, and yet be intellectually distinct from it, so that the object may be sought without regard to the pleasure involved.

Ordinary morality is clear that, when it aims at virtue for itself and others, it has not got its eye on wages or perquisites; its motive, in the sense of the object of its conscious desire, is not the anticipated feeling of pleasure. What it has before its mind is an object, an act or an event, which is not (for itself at least) a state of the feeling self, in itself or others. To say that, in desiring the right, it proposes to itself a pleasure to be got by the right, is to assert in the face of facts. To the moral mind that feeling is an accompaniment or a consequent, and it may be thought of as such. But to think of it as more, to propose it as the end to which the act or objective event are the means, and nothing but the means, is simply to turn the moral point of view upside down.—*Ibid.*, p. 85.

In this quotation is illustrated not only the sharp dichotomy between means and ends, but also the separation of an object from the feeling involved. Such a position could not be held if thinking were considered concretely, as it actually takes place. Empirically, to the question, do we seek an object or do we seek feelings, the only possible answer is that we seek both, and that they may be separated only in the mind, not in fact.

As a result of this initial theory, he is in a predicament when he faces the question of duty.

. . . we choose most certainly for ourselves (and so also for others) what we think the highest life, i.e. the life with the highest functions; and in that life we certainly include the feeling of pleasure; but if the alternative is presented to us of lower functions with less pains and greater pleasures, or higher functions with greater pains and less pleasures, then we must choose the latter.—*Ibid.,* p. 83.

To such a statement one is impelled to raise two questions. Why "must" we choose the greater pains and less pleasures? Bradley's answer, of course, would be that it was for the sake of self-realization. But why self-realization? And here there is no answer save a categorical statement that it is good. The other issue is concerned with the problem of how we are to know what the "highest functions" are. What is to be the criterion for deciding which functions are low and which are high?

If what he is concerned about is that men should not take the merely short view of life, desiring immediate pleasure, but should have a rational pattern for life, seeking that which would in the long run give the greatest happiness, there is little possibility of contradiction. At times this is what he seems to mean, but then he draws back lest thereby human responsibility and obligation be lost.

Obviously such premises lead to conclusions as to the place of punishment, which are far removed for those of the utilitarians. It is apparent that Bradley has little interest in the educational and social aspects. He does differentiate two kinds of punishment:

We must distinguish punishment and discipline, or correction; the former is inflicted because of wrong-doing, as desert, the latter is applied as means to improvement. It is right to inflict the former, only in the case of a being either wholly or partially accountable. The application of the latter (which is not punishment) is a practical question for parents or tutors, both in respect of the occasion and amount.—*Ibid.,* p. 29.

It is important to see that discipline with its implications for the individual and society is unimportant for him. He criticizes the utilitarian or determinist position sharply from this standpoint. For the necessitarian:

. . . there are two ends which are sufficient to justify punishment: the benefit of the offender himself, and the protection of others.

Necessitarianism fails in this, that it altogether ignores the rational self in the form of the will.—*Ibid.,* p. 30.

This is simply reiterating his distinction between the self, or will, and the character. The latter, being responsive to causes is legitimately subject to the utilitarian type of punishment which he calls discipline. Real punishment, however, for Bradley must be directed toward the will which is free.

It would seem that one possibility in such a position would be that this rational self or will was not so much in need of reforming as of informing. This would give a somewhat different trend to correction than that held by the utilitarians. But Bradley cannot accept such an attitude since it would, in the final analysis, remove the possibility of holding the individual accountable. In explicit terms he maintains that it is not ignorance but deliberate perversity which is responsible for evil.

It is false to say that evil is not done as evil; this or that evil act, when done, is desired for itself, and its content is known to be evil, and under the general head of evil is committed.—*Ibid.*, p. 273.

The essence of his philosophy is found in the attitude that if a man has a wrong will, *it is his fault*, morally if not physically.

No man can be tempted except by his own will; and the point is, Is it his fault that his will is not otherwise? If that is not his fault, then we admit that he was overborne—that volition was really impossible. But how many bad acts will this account of the matter excuse? Not many, we think.—*Ibid.*, ch. i.

Granting this view of guilt, he is compelled to take the position that "punishment is the denial of wrong, by the assertion of right." Any force used for education or reformation is mere discipline, to be left to parents and tutors. The philosopher is concerned with punishment as the defense of the abstract principle of right.

It would seem that with his stress on the self as being essentially rational he would take as his basis for morals standards arrived at through intellectual processes. Why he did not do so can only be a matter of conjecture. Perhaps he felt this was impossible without admitting feelings as normative; perhaps it was because he felt that, if it were an intellectual matter there would be room for error with the resulting inability to assess blame and responsibility. In any event he accepted completely the intuitive basis for morals: "That which tells us what in particular is right and wrong is not reflection but intuition." And in a footnote he makes clear what he means by it: " 'Intuitive' is here used as the opposite of 'reflective' or 'discursive,' 'intuition' as the opposite of 'reasoning' or 'explicit inferring.' "—*Ibid.*, ch. v.

In proof of his position he does not appeal to psychological inquiry or logical analysis; rather he finds the general belief to be sufficient evidence:

We prize the advice of persons who can give us no reasons for what they say. There is a general belief that the having a reason for all your actions is pedantic and absurd. There is a general belief that to try to have reasons for all that you do is sometimes very dangerous.—*Ibid.*, ch. v.

Obviously the result of such a position is to remove from the individual the necessity for thinking through his ethical problems. If it is "pedantic and absurd" or even "dangerous" to have a reason for your actions, then the simplest thing is to accept the conventions of society, and that is precisely what Bradley expects.

If a man is to know what is right, he should have imbibed by precept, and still more by example, the spirit of his community, its general and special beliefs as to right and wrong, and, with this whole embodied in his mind, should particularize it in any new case, not by a reflective deduction, but by an intuitive subsumption.—*Ibid.*, ch. v.

There is but one more step to take; that independent morality is wrong.

We should consider whether the encouraging oneself in having opinions of one's own, in the sense of thinking differently from the world on moral subjects, be not, in any person other than a heaven-born prophet, sheer self-conceit. And though the disease may spend itself in the harmless and even entertaining silliness by which we are advised to assert our social "individuality," yet still the having theories of one's own in the face of the world is not far from having practice in the same direction; and if the latter is (as it often must be) immorality, the former has certainly but stopped at the threshold.—*Ibid.*, ch. v.

As has been said before, it seems that his entire position is dominated by the need for placing responsibility. Unless he can categorically say: "You did wrong," and "you did it, not because there was an adequate cause or motive, but solely because you had a bad will," Bradley feels that there is no justification for morals or virtue. Over and over again he warns against any philosophy which will endanger the "possibility of imputation."

The above conclusions regarding the validity of punishment and its place in moral control are drawn from Bradley's *Ethical Studies*. Essentially that was the position which he continued to hold. He did, however, change his emphasis on retributive punishment. In the *International Journal of Ethics* for April 1894 he published an article on punishment in which there were some significant modifications.

It was the impact of the Darwinian theory of evolution which had caused him to rethink the question. The chief good remained, as it had been, the welfare of the community realized in its members. The means of achieving this good had changed, however. He recognized that if the evolutionary process were to continue constructively men would have to choose consciously their goals, that the community "must deliberately play its own Providence."

The major effect of this in the ethical realm was to break

the connection between punishment and guilt, and thereby weaken the retributive principle. If society were to be interested primarily in the task of determining its own future, it would have little time for the subleties involved in an accurate adjustment of punishment to guilt. It had not seemed so difficult formerly, but with a growing realization that at least some wrongdoing was the result of maladjustment it had become less easy to draw a line "between wilful badness and unwilled disease."

Bradley makes it quite clear that he still held "to the positive side of retributive punishment which declares punishment to be essentially the supplement of guilt." "But then this retributive view pure and simple will not work," and so he "made it secondary and subject to the chief end of the general welfare."

It would seem that this puts a fundamental contradiction between his theory and his practice. He is so concerned with the welfare of the community that it would almost seem as though he had become a convert to the doctrine of the greatest good for the greatest number. This is more evident when he makes explicit that he now regards punishment as "social surgery."

Darwinism, we may presume, should modify the view which we take of punishment. This does not mean that any of our old doctrines need quite be given up. The educational, the deterrent, and the retributive view may each retain, we may rather presume, a certain value. But all of these, it seems, must be in part superseded. They must be made subordinate to another and a higher law—what we may call the principle of social surgery. The right and the duty of the organism to suppress its undesirable growths is the idea of punishment directly suggested by Darwinism. It is an old doctrine which has but gained fresh meaning and force. And its principle is the old principle and the one ground for any sound theory of punishment. The moral supremacy of the community, its unrestricted right to deal with its members, is the sole basis on which rational punishment can rest.

He sums up his new emphasis in a striking sentence.

When justice (as it must be) is dethroned, and when Darwinism (as it will be) is listened to, there will be a favorable hearing for the claims of ethical surgery.

This conflict between his earlier theoretical basis and his later actual practice, he does not resolve. He apparently only partially realized that there was a fundamental dichotomy between punishment as retribution, which he sfill held though he had made it secondary, and punishment as social surgery, which he recognized as being the only practical approach. One wonders just what he meant when he said that none of the "old doctrines need *quite* be given up."

When one surveys his theoretical structure as a whole, the major impression is the way he illustrates how the theory of right and wrong can be divorced from the practical problems of discipline and control. He makes imputation of guilt a moral luxury, or end in itself, the essence of conscience; and separates such practice of praise and blame radically from any pedagogical devices for dealing with physical causes.

To this extent his position resembles that of Westermarck in opposition to the utilitarians. The question of whether morals are based on social intuitions (as is Bradley's view) or on emotions (as Westermarck held) is really of little practical importance. In either case, praise and blame are moral *ultimates,* not utilitarian instruments.

CHAPTER IV

MORAL JUDGMENTS AS EDUCATIONAL INSTRUMENTS FOR CONTROL

JOHN DEWEY (1859-   )

In turning from Green and Bradley to a study of the ethical theories of John Dewey, one meets a philosophy which has inherited much from those already discussed, and yet one which puts the whole problem of moral control in a fresh light. In each aspect of his thought it is the future which is of concern; the past is solely a deposit of experience for future use. "The moral issue concerns the future." In this respect he obviously resembles the utilitarians.

Central in Dr. Dewey's view of human nature is the place of habit. Bain had laid much stress on this interpretation, but he had given it no such all-important place. "Man is a creature of habit, not of reason nor yet of instinct." That sentence is the motif around which all Dr. Dewey's thought centers.

A habit is both a result and a cause. It is a reaction to what has preceded it and to what is around it. Or in other words: "habits are ways of using and incorporating the environment." In the second place a habit is "projective, dynamic." In taking such a position, Dr. Dewey has in mind those who believe that human nature is essentially passive, needing a stimulus from without to move it. It is such an attitude which he has in mind when he says:

... there is another assumption still more monstrous, namely, that man exists naturally in a state of rest so that he requires some external force to set him into action.—*Human Nature and Conduct*, p. 118.

The significance here, however, is that Dr. Dewey holds that not only the impulsive side of human nature is dynamic, but that habits which have usually been regarded as inherently static are equally projective. Habits are the self; *habits are the will.* Personality is not some mystic datum acquired at birth, but is purely the product of the organism interacting with its environment. "Character is the interpenetration of habits."

Starting with such a naturalistic premise it is no surprise to find him saying that: "For practical purposes morals mean customs, folkways, established collective habits." And again: "Customs in any case constitute moral standards." There is no divinely ordained moral code, no absolutes to be intuitively grasped. Morals spring up in precisely the same way as all other social customs and habits, and there is no mystery about why an individual holds the moral attitude that he does. "An individual usually acquires the morality as he inherits the speech of his social group." He inherits his morals as he does his manners and his physique.

This emphasis on the social nature of morality is reminiscent of Bradley. Dr. Dewey, however, breaks with the latter in making moral judgments instrumental rather than final. Moral codes thus inherited need continual revision. They exist as hypotheses with which constantly to experiment. They are programs of action steadily under fire, methods of inquiry requiring objective verification.

The problem of control for Dr. Dewey is the problem of

habit, or more accurately, the problem of the environment in which habits are incorporated. His attitude may fruitfully be contrasted with that of Green and Bradley. For them moral control was self-control. For Dr. Dewey as for the utilitarians, moral control is environmental control. It is inevitable that an ethic based on such a habit psychology should fix its attention upon the objective conditions in which habits are formed.

One of the important aspects of the problem of control is the question of the relation of motive to action. The issue has been especially acute since Bentham took the position that men were moved solely by pleasure and pain. Dr. Dewey breaks with this, accepting, with Bain, a dynamic psychology which holds that life is inherently active, and needs no motive to arouse it from passivity. A motive for him is a judgment taking place in the stream of activity giving direction to it:

An element in an act viewed as a tendency to produce such and such consequences is a motive. A motive does not exist prior to an act and produce it. It is an act plus a judgment upon some element of it, the judgment being made in the light of the consequences of the act.—*Ibid.*, p. 120.

In order to understand his position on this issue it is necessary to realize what he thinks the process of deliberation to be. Thinking starts with the awareness of a problem which has resulted from the blocking of some activity. At that point there is a mental, or rather an imaginative, rehearsal of all the possible courses of action. There is thus a genuine living through of various possibilities until one of them by its inherent attractiveness takes the field, and activity flows on unimpeded again. In the light of such a process it is clear what he means when he says that a motive is a judgment. The motive which directs the course of action is the judgment which has been passed as to which of the possible courses of action is most inherently attractive.

In discussing the question of motive, the problem raised by Bentham and others still remains: what are the ultimate springs of action, altruism, self-love, the search for happiness? Or as it is sometimes put: Is virtue to be sought as a means to happiness or as an end? Dr. Dewey cuts through a part of this discussion by pointing out that there is no sharp dichotomy between means and ends:

. . . ends, objectives, of conduct are those foreseen consequences which influence present deliberation and which finally bring it to rest by furnishing an adequate stimulus to overt action. . . They are not strictly speaking ends or termini of action at all. They are terminals of deliberation, and so turning points *in* activity.—*Ibid.,* p. 223.

Or as he puts it elsewhere: "Virtues are ends because they are such important means."

As one remembers how desperately Bradley struggled with this issue, feeling that when a virtue was practiced for any reason other than its own intrinsic good it was no longer a virtue, one wishes we might have his reply to Dr. Dewey's point that there is no sharp distinction between means and ends.

Granting this point, however, it is still significant to analyze more deeply the question of motivation. How are we to explain apparent self-inflicted pain and sacrifice? Bain had said that it was to be accounted for on the basis of habits which had been deliberately inculcated through the equating of social behavior with genuine satisfactions, which habits had persisted long after the specific stimulus was removed.

Dr. Dewey insists that living is its own end, and that it involves a false analysis to divide motives into altruistic and egoistic. There is ultimately but one category, life, which is its own end and its own justification. Inevitably all behavior is social.

Deliberate unscrupulous pursuit of self-interest is as much conditioned upon social opportunities, training and assistance as is the course of action prompted by a beaming benevolence.— *Ibid.*, p. 317.

Education is the ultimate moral process.

When we turn to Dr. Dewey's analysis of the specific instruments whereby moral control is to be achieved we find a clear recognition of how little knowledge education has at its disposal.

At present we not only have no assured means of forming character except crude devices of blame, praise, exhortation and punishment, but the very meaning of the general notions of moral inquiry is matter of doubt and dispute. The reason is that these notions are discussed in isolation from the concrete facts of the interactions of human beings with one another.— *Ibid.*, p. 324.

His attitude toward blame is what one would expect. Blame should not be retrospective or concerned with passing judgment, *save* as a means of learning for the future. "The reference in blame . . . is prospective, not retrospective."

He sees, as few writers in the ethical field, the dangers that are inherent in the use of blame. In the first place it is apt to blind our judgment:

The chief obstacle for example to recognizing the truth of a proposition frequently set forth in these pages to the effect that all conduct is potential, if not actual, matter of moral judgment is the habit of identifying moral judgment with praise and blame.—*Ibid., p.* 319.

That there is a real distinction between what is usually considered "blame" and what Dr. Dewey means by "moral judgment" seems obvious. Traditional *praise* and *blame* put morals into a separate category; *moral judgment* regards the logic of conduct as identical with the logic of thinking in general. Judgment is apt to be less heated than blame:

Judgment in which the emphasis falls upon blame and approbation has more heat than light. It is more emotional than intellectual. It is guided by custom, personal convenience and resentment rather than by insight into causes and consequences. —*Ibid., p.* 320.

Dr. Dewey makes much of the fact of contingency, and it is important to see both what this does and does not involve. Metaphysically it means that this is the kind of universe where things are not "fixed, settled once for all," and where choice is, therefore, possible. The assumption is sometimes made that this is a defence of psychological indeterminism. Dr. Dewey is far from holding such a belief. He insists that indeterminism is not contingency; it is mere chance.

It is this demand for genuine contingency which is caricatured in the orthodox doctrine of a freedom of indifference, a power to choose this way or that apart from any habit or impulse, without even a desire on the part of will to show off.—*Human Nature and Conduct, p.* 309.

Freedom, then, is not "free will." It is not turning our backs on an empirical world; it is not removing the will from the realm of causal sequences. The exact reverse is the fact. We have freedom *because* we do not have psychological indeterminism, *because* this is a world where the rule of cause and effect is universal.

We are told that seriously to import empirical facts into morals is equivalent to an abrogation of freedom. Facts and laws mean necessity we are told. The way to freedom is to turn our back upon them and take flight to a separate ideal realm . . . the road to freedom may be found in that knowledge of facts which enables us to employ them in connection with desires and aims. A physician is free in his thought and his action in the degree in which he knows what he deals with.— *Human Nature and Conduct,* p. 303.

Nor does Dr. Dewey cease at this point. He analyzes the values which men have sought in their search for freedom. He feels that it is the capacity to deal effectively with situations without feeling that one is a pawn in the hands of fate. Men have thought that the only way to preserve these values was by insisting on indeterminism.

What men have esteemed and fought for in the name of liberty is varied and complex—but certainly it has never been a metaphysical freedom of will. It seems to contain three elements of importance, though on their face not all of them are directly compatible with one another. (1) It includes efficiency in action, ability to carry out plans, the absence of cramping and thwarting obstacles. (2) It also includes capacity to vary plans, to change the course of action, to experience novelties. And again (3) it signifies the power of desire and choice to be factors in events.—*Human Nature and Conduct,* p. 303.

Dr. Dewey accepts these values as genuine, but insists that they are lost in any metaphysical freedom of the will; indeterminism makes one a mere automaton.

Freedom, then, is not the result of indeterminism, it is a

quality of intelligent action. It is based, not on its *antecedents,* but on its *consequences;* it is prospective, not retrospective. The free man is the intelligent one. "Intelligence is the key to freedom in action."

To revert to his doctrine of contingency, this is the kind of universe where choices have to be made, i.e., where intelligence is demanded. Deliberation is required "not because it (the world) is inherently vacillating and unstable, but because deliberation and choice are determining and stabilizing factors."

There will be some who will feel that this is not freedom since the intelligence is determined. Dr. Dewey is quite explicit in acknowledging this; intelligence is determined by its motives. But here again, one must remember that the test is not retrospective. The issue is not whether choice is made apart from specific conditions, but is it made wisely? Freedom is intelligent choice, not undetermined choice.

We are free in the degree in which we act knowing what we are about. The identification of freedom with "freedom of will" locates contingency in the wrong place. Contingency of will would mean that uncertainty was uncertainly dealt with; it would be a resort to chance for a decision.—*The Quest for Certainty,* p. 250.

The importance of all this lies in the fact that on this basis responsibility becomes profoundly real; real not because of any antecedents, but because people inevitably *hold us* responsible. Society says quite definitely that it likes or dislikes our behavior. No claim of ignorance or irresponsibility on our part makes others feel otherwise. Consciously or unconsciously, it is recognized that holding people responsible makes them responsible, i.e., changes their attitude. At this point Dr. Dewey is very close to the utilitarian position.

The individual is *held* accountable for what he *has* done in order that he may be responsive in what he is *going* to do. Gradually persons learn by dramatic imitation to hold themselves accountable, and liability becomes a voluntary deliberate acknowledgment that deeds are our own, that their consequences come from us.—*Human Nature and Conduct*, p. 316.

Responsibility becomes, thus, practically, rather than metaphysically, justified. We become responsible, i.e., responsive, because society requires it. To be *responsible* for our acts is to be *answerable* for them.

As one evaluates Dr. Dewey's total position it becomes clear on the one hand how much he owes to those who have preceded him, but also, on the other hand, how genuinely new a synthesis he has made.

He has maintained the spirit of early utilitarianism, while refining it by means of the more penetrating psychology of Bain, and the general criticism of Green. For example, in his theory of moral judgment he is in the utilitarian stream when he makes judgment instrumental, not final; prospective, not based on metaphysical accountability. He reflects the idealistic attitude, however, in making judgment inherent, not a system of external sanctions imposed by society.

Perhaps his most significant departure from Green and Bradley was to discard the idea of transcendental self, and substitute a self which is purely the result of physical and social forces. There is for him no separate psychic realm, no self cut off from its natural environment. Human nature, personality, is as much a part and product of its environment as is a plant.

Finally, he has gone beyond all previous ethical theorists, in recognizing the need for a method of analyzing "the obscure and usually unavowed forces" which lie behind human activity.

PART TWO

A STUDY OF THE DEVELOPMENT OF
RESPONSIBILITY IN TWELVE
CHILDREN

CASE REPORTS

Hugh Carr

The significance of the case of Hugh Carr lies more in its picture of the causes that lay back of his behavior problems and the ineffectiveness of the punishments which were used, than for any marked success of the other methods tried.

He was a boy eight years old when he was referred to the doctors. His conduct at school was entirely beyond the teachers' control. His mother said he was moody and disobedient at home, stubborn and given to whining. Much time was spent in investigating the attitude of his parents and teachers. It was clear that his father was inconsistent in his attitude toward the boy. When Hugh was stubborn, or whined, or refused to obey, the father became nervous and irritated, his temper flashed up, he grabbed the boy, punished him, and then half an hour later apparently had forgotten all about it. To him, Hugh was just a spoiled child. He regarded his conduct as absolutely unexplainable, except for the fact that he was just plain mean, and he was at a loss to know why punishing him so severely had had no effect. At times, if Hugh kept whining and teasing for something, his father would give it to him in order to quiet him. His mother, too, could not understand why punishment seemed to do him no good. She related one instance in which she beat him until her mother-in-law pulled him away from her, and still he did not seem to realize that he had done anything wrong. She felt that his behavior was due to a desire to have his own way.

When an investigation was made of his early childhood, it was discovered that he had given no trouble until when he was two years old, he had made a visit to his grandmother. It was after his return from this visit that he first showed signs of obstinacy and temper tantrums when he did not get what he wanted. These reactions were aggravated when the family moved to New Jersey to live with the paternal grandparents. This household was crowded with both adults and children. The mother explained that she did not feel free to do as she chose in that house and that she could not prevent the other adults from spoiling Hugh. When she did punish him and the others thought it was not justified, they would take his part. Often, when he got into trouble with the other children, she would spank him in order to avoid conflict and irritation with the other members of the family, although it might not have been his fault. Since that time, his stubbornness, lying, etc., increased in spite of the direst punishments they could think of.

His teacher said that Hugh had almost wrecked her health that year. She had exhausted every device she could think of to manage him, but without effect. She tried ignoring him, thinking that this would bring him around, but he was perfectly contented just to make himself obnoxious in other ways. When she gave him something to do, he stubbornly refused to do it, or else whined. In the past, he used to call his teacher names of such vileness as to beggar description, but he had stopped that since the principal threatened to expel him. They put him into a lower class to punish him and put him into a more advanced class to inspire him, without any effect. He had to be dropped from the gymnasium because he made life miserable for everyone and effectively stopped the progress of the class.

Another teacher said that she had tried everything: praise, letting him do special errands, making him a monitor, giving him responsibility; that she would meet him in the hall, put her arms around him and say, "Now, aren't you going to be a good boy so that you can be a captain?" He would declare that he would be good and in ten minutes he would be raising pandemonium. She said he lied like a trooper. He absolutely defied her and it was necessary for her to send for his father. Both the father and mother were so exasperated with his conduct that they were at a loss to know what to do. In fact, his mother said to the doctor that if he would call up and tell her that Hugh had been run over and killed, she would go down on her knees and thank God.

Some time previously, his mother had had difficulty with Hugh's picking up money about the house and spending it for candy. She tried to be more careful about leaving money around, with the result that Hugh had shown no more tendency to take things. He persisted, however, in lying. Even after punishment, he still stoutly insisted that he was telling the truth. He never seemed penitent or sorry and did not realize the justice of any punishment. If he had to go to bed without his supper, he would simply cry and whine and no amount of persuasion could bring him to see that he was being punished in this way. The mother and father exhausted every known means of punishment. They sent him to bed. They deprived him of desserts. They whipped him unmercifully. They shamed him and humiliated him before others by telling of his misdeeds. The week he was suspended from school, he was not allowed to go outside during the whole time and was not permitted to play with any of his playthings. Every visitor who came in was told how terribly he had behaved and what a disgrace he was, but the combined effect of all this was not sufficient to make him volunteer to apologize to the teacher when he returned. It was only through dire threats of continued punishment that he was induced to ask forgiveness.

When he first visited the doctor, he appeared to be a well-built, healthy boy. Although he wore an almost constant scowl, his features frequently lighted up with an alert smile. It was soon found that the scowl was only superficial and could be easily chased away by any kindness or humor.

When the doctor inquired into the cause of his trouble at school, he replied in a rather bragging manner, "Some of the kids at school think I can't fight. The very toughest came up to me and said, 'Do you want to fight?' and gave me a biff, and I gave him a bang of an uppercut and down he went. When he got up, I said, 'Do you want to fight?' and he said, 'I quit,' and he ran for home." Hugh continued to talk in this bragging manner of his numerous fights and conquests at school and said, "The boys call me names and say I am only a show-off, but I run after them and bang them." The doctor inquired what happened when all this fighting went on at school; to which he replied cheerfully, "Oh, I go to the office every day," and then added, "Our teacher has headaches every minute almost, is always talking about them, and she goes out of the classroom and we go over the desks, and then you should hear her yell at us."

He was asked why the other boys picked on him, to which he answered, "Because they're tough." The doctor gained the impression that he was looking for special attention from his teacher, especially as he was so susceptible to every bit of affection which was shown him. When he was appealed to on a "a real boy" basis, he smiled appreciatively and at once became agreeable. His last remark was, "Sure I can be good at school."

When he was given his physical examination, he persisted in pulling away, even before the doctor touched him. The doctor spoke quietly to him, explaining that he was not playing, but still the boy would not let himself be touched. Thinking to see what his attitude would be when forced to obey, the doctor held firmly until he had finished his examination. As soon as this happened, Hugh started to cry at the top of his lungs, but no attention was paid him, and the examination was carried out. When it was finished, Hugh sat up and immediately smiled, showing no resentment whatever. The doctor asked him why he had made such a noise, to which he answered, "I didn't want you to touch me. That's the way I do." And when asked if that was what he always did, he answered with a smile, "Yes, but it didn't work this time." He came back to the doctor some weeks later, telling him with pride how much better he was behaving. The doctor made the remark, "Well, that's growing up, isn't it?" He added that he was sure in time Hugh would get rid of all his babyish behavior. Suddenly the boy asked, "Don't you think I'm talking better?" He certainly was, for during that visit, he did not assume a whining tone once.

He did speak in a complaining manner of his sister, saying. "Mary always wants to tag about with me, even when I go on my bike. I wish she would go and play by herself and leave a fellow alone. This morning when I spoke to her, she told me to mind my own business, and she made a face at me, too. I know I would be better off if she weren't here." It seemed that perhaps the boy's jealousy of his sister was caused, in part at least, by the very marked attention which she got from her parents.

The limitations of his environment were an important factor, as there were few children to play with and his mother kept continual supervision over him. It was decided first, therefore, to try to influence the parents to move to a more desirable neighborhood; second, to interpret to the parents the meaning of Hugh's behavior, showing them his need for more friendly attention and enlisting their coöperation in helping him achieve a more mature attitude; third, to secure the assistance of the school in getting him opportunities for making a place for himself; fourth, if possible, to find a camp where he could go during the summer.

The first of these plans proved to be a failure, as the family could not afford to move. It was difficult to give the parents any fundamental understanding of the boy, and it was apparent they could not accept any constructive suggestions for his treatment. They persisted in punishing him, without regard to the effectiveness of the punishment. They could not realize that if at the age of eight years, Hugh was beyond the control of everyone, they, as his parents, had a certain responsibility for that condition. They could only see him as a thoroughly bad boy who willfully refused to behave himself for no reason at all except innate meanness.

For this reason, it was considered all the more imperative that he be sent to camp in order that he might get out of the situation where he was competing with his sister and where his parents kept him on an infantile level. It was necessary for him to go where there would be an emphasis upon his growing up. He did not make a success of his first camp venture and was sent home after a few days. His mother took the attitude that he would have to be punished severely, no matter what the cause of his trouble at camp had been. Her one and only answer to all suggestions was, "Of course, he could have helped it. He just didn't want to behave, and after all we've done for him, he doesn't appreciate anything." He was sent to another camp, however, and there he seemed to make a satisfactory adjustment.

As soon as he returned home, however, his problems recurred and it was finally decided that he must be sent away to school. The last report was that he was doing satisfactory work and was popular with the other boys. The doctor went up to see him and found him much improved. Details are lacking as to why he made this adjustment, but it was apparent that the situation was very different from that to which he had been accustomed.

ALLEN HOBART

Allen Hobart was eight years old when his mother brought him to the doctor to ask for assistance in handling him, saying that she could not manage him. He was disobedient, smoked, and stole. His family situation was found to be about as bad as it could be. When his father was irritated, he scolded the boy, used a rough domineering tone, and whipped him severely.

Mrs. Hobart was thoroughly inconsistent in her attitude. She talked in a high-pitched voice and appeared to be easily irritated by the children. She said she had a bad temper and had no control of it. When angry, she became half-crazed and was apt to whip her children unmercifully. In handling them, she wanted unquestioned obedience. When Allen did not obey her, she became overwrought because her will was being crossed. She thought she had inherited her temper from her father, and for this reason considered it part of her nature and unchangeable.

She felt that Allen intentionally tormented her and that he got a real "kick" out of being devilish, as she explained it. At times, his conduct had so irritated her that she had bitten him on the cheek and made it black and blue. She thought that he was ashamed of his conduct and feared the punishment.

She felt ashamed of herself to have such a boy. She said she had done everything for him, giving him money whenever he wanted it, giving him good food, keeping his clothes in condition, and still he disobeyed her. She recognized that she had made no progress with her methods of discipline.

There was no question but that Allen was stubborn. When he said he would not do something, he gritted his teeth and no matter how hard he was whipped, he would not give in. He seemed to like to torment his mother and would show no emotion when he was being punished. Instead, he would say, "You can't hurt me."

The problem seemed hopeless from the beginning, as the mother said she could not control her temper. She was willing to try anything to correct him, but said that he irritated her so much, she could make no promises. The doctor urged the parents not to whip the boy, since it was obviously doing no good. If he had to be impressed with his wrongdoing, they should give him only five cents a week for allowance or forbid him to go to the movies or send him to bed without a story. If he cried, they were not to relent, but to let him cry it out.

The boy had been kept very much of a child, not even

being allowed to dress himself. He had not made an attempt to wash his face and hands until very recently. The doctor showed him how to dress and wash himself and he seemed really anxious to learn. He was very pleased when commended on his success. It seemed impossible to persuade his mother to persist in some definite course of action. An illustration of this occurred one evening when Allen refused to eat his dinner. His father sent him to bed without it. About nine o'clock, Mr. and Mrs. Hobart were having tea in the kitchen. Allen called out and said he wanted some, but his father refused since he had not been willing to eat his dinner. Mrs. Hobart, however, said that he ought not to have to go to sleep hungry and so gave him some cake. Another incident which indicated her method of handling him was the following: Allen awakened early one morning, dressed himself alone, and went to his mother's bed and told her to get up. She scolded him for arising so early, told him to undress and go back to bed. When he was awakened later to go to school, Mrs. Hobart dressed him, even though she had had proof that he could do it alone.

Some weeks later, his mother admitted that she was continuing to baby him. She said that though she had refused him an allowance for that week, later she had given him money for the movies. The doctor pointed out the futility of this, but she replied. "He screams and kicks when I don't." The doctor told her that she should put him in a room alone and let him cry as long as he wished. She burst out, "You think I can be calm and nice to anyone like him. I can never like him. He drives me crazy." This seemed appallingly true, as was illustrated by her attitude when Allen ventured to argue with her. She became infuriated and said,

"You shut up or I'll hit you on the mouth." Allen shrank back and tears came into his eyes. Another time, when Allen said that his mother had not allowed him to go out, she became furious, saying, "Did you say I wouldn't let you go?" He replied, "Yes, I wanted to go and you wouldn't let me." He then began to cry. She screamed, "You little liar. I'd like to choke you. What won't I do to you when I have you alone!"

There was no question but that Allen had given his mother great provocation. At one time, when she refused him some request, he tipped over his milk, shoved all his food on the tablecloth and kicked the table until she screamed with irritation. Mr. Hobart commented at this point that when she screamed, a gleam of satisfaction appeared on the boy's face. He said, "It is apparent that he deliberately devils his mother." The doctor tried to point out that if she had not screamed, Allen would have been defeated and she would have been the victor.

The parents were urged to pursue the following course: first, not to whip him, as it was obviously futile, but to use some more humane form of punishment; second, not to pamper him in food fads or give in to his whims; third, Mrs. Hobart was especially urged to control her own temper so that she should not give the boy the satisfaction of making her angry; finally, the parents were urged to be consistent in punishments and rewards.

It became more and more obvious that the mother was the real problem, and that Allen's difficulties could not be solved until she gained more insight and control over herself. This seemed so impossible that an attempt was made to see what could be accomplished through working with his school. His teacher gave him a chart and a box of gold stars and he was told to put one on for every day that he behaved. A week later, he proudly exhibited six stars. The doctor praised him for his good work and told him he could get a fine record next time. Some weeks later, he brought the chart back, proudly exhibiting the gold stars, and even his mother admitted they had been deserved.

At school, he was given the leading part in a play and he showed considerable dramatic ability. This greatly pleased his mother, who said, "Gosh, I was proud of him. They got him up on the platform afterwards and hand-clapped him. I was some proud to be his mother that time." Up to this time, there had been great evidence of his improvement, both at home and in school, largely because of the encouragement that had been given him by the doctor and his teacher. Two weeks later, however, he seemed to have completely regressed. He was more impudent than ever and thoroughly unmanageable. The doctor tried to discover what the cause was and asked his mother what she thought. The latter replied, "I suppose you think it's me that caused it, but I didn't. He's just a devil, that's all. He shrugs his shoulders when I speak to him and mutters and snarls and I get so mad I see red, and I pound him until, if my husband or mother didn't pull me off, I'd kill him." It seemed that it had all started over some minor incident for which he was severely punished. From then on, he had gone from bad to worse.

Realizing that there was no hope for the boy so long as he remained in that environment, he was taken out of the home and sent to a camp, where he seemed to be contented and adjusted. When he came home that fall, the doctor talked to him at some length about the new situation, telling him that he could now make a clean record for himself, that he was a bright boy with all the qualifications for success, and that he had reached the age where he would have to renounce his baby ways. Allen admitted that and said he wanted to grow up. The case, however, was very far from being a success. It was impossible to remove him permanently from his home, and until that was done there could be but little hope for him.

Donald Morio

In May, 1926, Donald Morio was referred by a Mr. Johnson because of thefts in his office amounting to about $36.00. Before he was referred, every effort had been made to handle the situation. When the thefts were first discovered, Donald seemed extremely penitent and was given every chance to make good, but he became more and more careless in his work, staying away frequently. At home he had also become a serious problem, striking his mother and sisters, staying out nights, and gambling. When an investigation was made of his family situation, it was found that his father and mother had separated. His elder sister, Mary, seemed very decidedly to be the most dependable person in the family. Donald himself said of her at one time, "My big sister, Mary, is like you. She doesn't say people are just bad and want to be. She tries to understand and help them like you do."

His brother, John, had also been a problem, having stayed away from school, and having been on probation for a time. There was chronic warfare between Donald and John, and the latter's domination was vigorously resented.

Donald's most recent difficulty dated from the time when he had secured a steady position. At first he had done well, being quick to understand. Later he had learned to use the telephone switchboard. In July, $10.00 was missing from the cash box. Two months later the telephone operater reported having missed money upon three different occasions. This continued until at least $35.00 was stolen. Donald finally admitted that he was responsible for the thefts and promised that he would pay back what he had taken. He gradually lost interest in his work, however, and finally was dismissed from his position.

His own story of the difficulty was as follows: "My crowd used to play baseball for $5.00 and a league ball a game, the team winning to get these. That meant that each of us had to put in seventy cents a week. I was catcher and had to have a body protector as well. We always played up town and had to pay our own way, and then a fellow gets thirsty and has to have a drink once in a while. All the other fellows had money but I never had enough to pay my share. One day after I had been at the office for only a few weeks, I saw some money. I don't know how much. It seemed a lot to me and I took about $3.00. Then later when the girls would go upstairs and leave their pocketbooks in their desks, it was so easy I just kept on taking."

After telling this Donald sat quiet for a time as if studying something. When asked what would have happened if he had gone and told these people he needed the money to play baseball, he said, "I know they would have given it to me but I couldn't tell them. I hated to tell anyone how poor we were."

When asked if he was satisfied that he had done his part

to rectify fully his mistake, he said, "No, I have not, I still owe $6.00 and I mean to pay it."

One month after he had made his first contacts with the doctor, he came into the office appearing somewhat embarrassed. As he entered he did not smile as he had at other times, but sat quietly in a chair. He had by this time secured another position in a hat store and the doctor asked him how the business was. At this the boy showed some confusion and said, looking directly at the doctor, "I was laid off last Thursday." When asked what the reason was, with bowed head he said, "I tried to take a cap and they got it. A new stock of nice caps had just come in. They were expensive ones and I took one down stairs and hid it behind a box, but the boss found it and said he would have to let me go."

A little later he added, "It was all my own fault, I shouldn't have tried to take it. I could have gotten one from them at wholesale price if I could have afforded it, but I couldn't. Mother's hard up now."

It was obvious that he had a very deep feeling of guilt. The doctor discussed the situation with him, not on a basis of trying to shame him but on the basis of childhood versus manhood reactions, and Donald gradually lost much of his hang-dog expression. The doctor told him that he believed he was capable of a more mature attitude and assured him of his belief that he could handle this situation in a manly fashion.

The next time Donald came to the doctor's office, he appeared much upset as though he were ready to cry. When asked what the matter was he said, "John went and spilled the beans to mother, he went and told her everything." He then added that his mother was greatly upset and would not even speak to him, and he asked if someone from the doctor's office could go over to talk with her. When questioned further as to his mother's attitude, he said, "All she did was shame me and said she didn't see how I could come over here and face you, but she doesn't know you and how you talk."

He was feeling very badly humiliated. The doctor tried to cheer him, yet drew attention to the fact that in reality he was responsible for the present situation. Donald accepted the responsibility and said, "If I can get another chance, I will show them I am no crook."

The doctor continued the discussion with Donald later, talking over with him many of the processes of growing up, showing him that manhood consists of more than mere bulk of body or even of education. He stressed the necessity of growing up emotionally as well as other ways. Donald seemed to grasp the significance of the discussion for he later remarked, "I know lots of men and women who still are acting like children."

Because his sister Mary occupied so large a part in his life, the doctor decided to talk over the situation with her, and had her come to his office. He stressed the fact that she could be of real service in influencing Donald, telling her how it was understood nowadays that misconduct on the part of children, lying or stealing, was not in itself the trouble with the boy, but represented his attempt to solve other problems, and that it was these other problems that they had to face. He compared this attitude as analogous to the theory of physical illness. For example, in typhoid fever there was a high temperature, but, when the physician was called, he did not attempt to treat this condition but recognized it to be only a symptom of another condition. The same he said was true of Donald's behavior. It would do no good to nag him continually about his conduct. The cause must be found and conditions changed so that he would no longer need to act in this fashion.

The doctor pointed out that what Donald needed most was to feel that the other members of the family accepted him on an adult basis and let him share their responsibility. As long as they let Donald feel that they did not expect any better conduct from him, and failed to put any premium on the good things he did, he would not put forth much effort to do differently. They ought to ignore his bad conduct and praise the good things he did, so he would feel that his good conduct was appreciated.

Mary was inclined to deprecate her influence, saying that she had talked and talked to him but it did not seem to do any good. The doctor asked whether she had ever taken any one habit that was disagreeable to her, and worked with him specifically on it, or whether she had generalized her efforts about his bad conduct. She admitted that she had never tried to work out anything specific with him. The doctor suggested that she now try to take just one offensive habit and discuss it with him, pointing out the desirability of change, and, without unduly condemning him for the habit, make him feel she would approve a change. Thereafter she should take care to ignore his mistakes, specially notice his good deeds, and see what effect it would have on him. He pointed out that, when anyone was overburdened as Donald then was, to have all his faults held up to him at once was overpowering and tended to crush any self-confidence he might have in his ability to overcome them, but that to take just one thing, concentrate on it, and show him he could do it, would give him a sense of success and gradually build up his desire to overcome more and more in order to win approval and confidence thereby. He told her it did no good to approve of a few things, unless at the same time the majority of the undesirable things were ignored.

After careful examination of the boy's capacity, it was decided that he would be more successful were he to leave school at this point, since he was sixteen years of age, and take a position preferably where he could use his mechanical aptitude.

The decision to get a position marked an important step in the boy's development, for it gave the opportunity of bringing clearly before him the implications of what he had done before. The doctor insisted that when asked why he had been dismissed from previous jobs, Donald tell the truth and admit that he had stolen. He was also to give the doctor's name as a reference so the latter could testify as to his belief that the boy was going to be honest in the future.

It was difficult to find employment with his record, but a man was finally discovered who was willing to take him on trial, and let Donald prove "that he was no crook."

He continued to see the doctor at frequent intervals, talking over with him his problems and apparently getting both insight and confidence from him. It was also apparent that his sister, Mary, had coöperated very intelligently in helping the boy, especially with new habits. It was just a year later that he came into the doctor's office and when asked how he was getting along, replied, "I think I am doing fairly well. The other day I was introduced to the President along with

some others. Now I almost feel I am one of the Company."
The boy had made his adjustment and the case was closed.

FRANK MORRISSEY

At ten years of age Frank Morrissey was referred to the
doctor as a boy who refused to do any work and who had
violent fits of temper. He had been suspended from school
finally because of a temper tantrum in which the teacher
feared for the safety of the other children.

His teacher said that his conduct had become worse and
worse. He was destructive, often getting up in the middle of
the classroom, snatching a child's pencil and breaking it into
pieces. He would knock his desk with his knees, making
such a noise that it was difficult to conduct the class. Whenever she turned her back, he would take the opportunity of
hitting someone, even though there was no apparent cause.
He had violent fits of temper, in which he kicked, bit, and
fought. There were times when he would be docile or try
to amuse the other students, but he would pass quickly from
a jovial mood into a fierce outbreak. She said she had tried
every means of disciplining him without success. He had
kept conduct books for a few days and then lost interest.
Isolation in a seat away from the other students kept him
in order for only a short time, as he would leave his seat and
run across the room if he wanted to hit someone. Some days
she could tell by his wild-eyed expression that he would become disturbed by the first thing which crossed him. One
day he stamped into the room with his big boots on. Some
of the boys began calling him Charlie Chaplin, the Crazy.
After she had ignored his repeated requests for recognition,
he became furious and began kicking and striking his ad-

versaries. As he looked like "a wild animal," she thought there was no place for him in the schoolroom and sent for his mother to take him home.

On investigating the family situation, it was found that his father had a terrific temper. He was not easily excited, but when the children became bothersome, he got in such a state that he hit them and knocked them about. His antagonism toward Frank was more apparent than toward the other children, as he said Frank was noisier around the house and apt to be quarrelsome. Frank's own story of the difficulty, as he told it to the doctor, was as follows: "Well, I guess I was having too much trouble. I was a bad kid and I know it. The trouble was I was very bad in 3B. The boys used to call me crazy. They used to call me Charlie Chaplin. I told them not to and I pinched and hit them, but I'm not so very strong. Do you think I'm strong? I wish I could be strong." He did not blame his teachers for his troubles, saying that they were nice to him. "They just get sick and terribly tired of me when I don't obey them. They are nice and I'm going to try to be good after this, but I tell you I'm not strong. I don't look strong when I take my clothes off to take a bath at night. I'm not strong. Could you do anything about it?"

It was apparent that this problem of getting to be strong preoccupied him almost exclusively. "I like all kinds of games where they make you run and get strong. The teacher what came to my house said she will get me into the Boy Scouts. I would like to be a Scout, so I could get strong. I feel I am weak and I cannot say I am great in anything. My cousin says sometime he is going to take me up to Pelham Bay and put me into training. He says he will give me a glass of milk, then take me for a good long walk, then have me rest and take a swim. That's what I'd like to do, get strong."

In dealing with the mother, the doctor urged her not to speak of Frank as a bad boy in his presence, but to praise him for his good behavior and tell the other children how well he was turning out. The type of discipline which consisted largely of yelling and threatening had obviously brought no results. It was pointed out that both she and her husband would have to control themselves if they expected to keep the children in check. She was urged to be firm and positive in her dealings with them, but on no account to lose her temper or to make threats which she did not intend to carry out.

The afternoon that Frank's teacher, Miss Smith, was interviewed, the boy was found to be having some difficulty. He had come to class without a necktie and Miss Smith had pinned a paper tie on him and made him stand before the class. She said that on the whole his behavior had been good this semester. Had she not been told by a previous teacher that he was exceedingly troublesome and given to temper attacks, she would not have thought him a problem case, as there were several boys who were more difficult to handle. She was told that Frank had said that he thought his teacher liked him and that he was doing better work because he knew she did not think him bad. It was suggested to her that since he did feel he had her confidence, that if she continued to show that she thought well of him, he would continue to try to please her.

Because of Frank's absorbing desire to become stronger, the doctor endeavored to deal with this situation as a necessary step in the boy's social adjustment. He prescribed

glandular medicine in order to stimulate his growth and rec-
ommended a diet. Frank returned to the doctor some weeks
later and said with a show of great importance that he had
been taking the pills regularly and wished to have more. In
his own words, "I'm growing big and tall and I'm acting
more like a man."

This behavior lasted for some time, until he was reported
once more for misbehavior at school. It was found then
that he had been given another teacher, and that it was she
who had said he was behaving so disgracefully. The doctor
tried to explain Frank's misbehavior on the ground of recent troubles in his home, but his teacher replied that this
could not possibly be the reason. She took the doctor to the
classroom where Frank had been given a special chair right
next to her desk. It was apparent that she used high-handed
methods with her pupils, scolding and threatening them constantly. She kept talking about his failings in front of the
class and when the doctor suggested that this might harm
him, she said loudly that nothing affected him at all, as he
was entirely hardened to everything.

Further investigation revealed the fact that the trouble
had originally started when Frank had got into a quarrel
with one of his classmates. The cause was obscure, but the
teacher had certainly blamed Frank and had sent for his
mother. When his mother went to the school, the teacher
had persuaded her to beat her son with a ruler before the
entire class. From then on, he was unquestionably incorrigible.

The doctor discussed this latter difficulty with Frank, sug-
gesting that he not hit the children no matter what they did
to him, and that he wait at least until after school was over

if he had any fighting to do. The doctor also suggested that perhaps his teacher would be nice to him if he stopped annoying her.

When summer came, to his intense delight an opportunity was found for him to go to a camp, where all his dreams were realized. There he spent his whole time in "getting strong," and the attempt to do that kept him so busy that there seemed to be no time for him to get into trouble.

His mother came slowly to realize how little affection he had had at home. Her change in attitude was made evident when it was found out he was not going to pass at school. She seemed to understand that a repetition of the present grade would give him a chance to be more successful later on, and above all, she saw what harm might be done to him if displeasure and punishment were visited upon him as a result. In fact, she explained the situation to his father so that the latter would not be angry.

The following year he had a teacher whom he liked, perhaps because as he said, "She likes me." He was chosen one of four pupils of the class to speak in the auditorium, which he did very well. His work was so good that he seemed capable of getting along in a higher grade, but it was decided that promotion at that time of the year might disturb the adjustment he had made, as another teacher might not handle him satisfactorily.

Four months later, word was sent to the doctor that he had been in trouble again. His mother described the difficulty as follows: He had come home from school one night acting as though he were sick. She finally asked if something were troubling him and he told her that at recess he had seen a school paint box on the hall floor. His first thought was to take it back to the room at once, but he decided he would not be expected to go back to the room then, so he slipped it into his coat pocket with the idea of giving it to the teacher as soon as he returned. But he forgot it while he was out and soon after returning to the room, while taking some exercise, the box fell out of his pocket to the floor. He was immediately accused of being a thief and of having stolen the box. He asked his mother to go to the school to see his teacher. She went the next morning and was told there was no definite proof he had stolen it, and that he would not be further punished. His mother believed he had told the truth, but it was, of course, impossible to be certain.

His only other difficulty came late that spring. He had done well in school all year and his teacher had given him a grade of B constantly. The last month, however, she had given him C in conduct, because she thought it might encourage him to do better and she promised to give him a B again this month if he were more quiet. She said he was not a bad boy, but that he was constantly doing something to draw the attention of the other children. When he received his report, he became angry with her, called her names and said he would tear up the report. He did not come to school on Monday. Tuesday his mother came with him, saying he had not come because of the low grade and that she would have to bring him every day or he would not come. The situation was explained to his teacher and she realized the effect the lower grade had had upon him when he had been trying so hard to get her confidence. The suggestion was made to her that he would need much patience and she responded cordially.

The following year his adjustment at school seemed to be

satisfactory. Frank said that he had a good teacher and that his work was going well. He had had some little trouble with another boy in the class, but had asked to have his seat changed and had got along well since then. During the weekends, he was caddying and got much pleasure from it. The school had no further complaints to make.

SIDNEY SHARP

Sidney Sharp was eleven years old when he was referred to the doctors because of his heedlessness and carelessness, as well as for stealing. The situation came to a head when, with a few companions, he broke into a store. The boys were taken to court, but the charge was not pressed.

Sidney had seven brothers and sisters, with whom he seemed to get along pretty well, except one sister, Ruth, who was two years older than he. She apparently tried to dominate him, which caused intense resentment on his part. His mother felt that his behavior was something to be ashamed of and that it might be a punishment from God. Speaking of his father, Sidney remarked, "Father is always hollering at me. He has always done it. He doesn't holler at Ruth hardly at all." When asked why, he said, "He thinks more of her and is kind to her. If she has anything to tell on me, she tells father, because she knows he will strap me. Sometimes he gets mad and hits me on the head with the strap. He sometimes punches me on the head with his fists. About two months ago he hit me with his fists and knocked me unconscious." When asked what his mother thought of this, he replied, "She is glad, so as to make me good." He was asked if he thought it would make him good, to which he answered. "I don't think that's the way." But he could not tell of a better way.

His teacher said that she thought he was a lovable boy who had good intentions but was easily led into mischief. His school work had suffered because of his lack of drill in a previous school. She said that when he was punished for slamming the door or making unnecessary noise, he appeared most ashamed and never sulked. She said that his chief fault lay in trying to attract attention by giggling, teasing the other children, or in some other way.

Sidney's story of the time when he was caught stealing was as follows: He was skating on the sidewalk and met a boy slightly younger than himself who related to him how he had got into several places and obtained candy and money. He urged Sidney to go with him so that he could have some of the things for himself. He explained that all they had to do was to climb up on a certain roof, lift the skylight and drop in, and then come back the same way. They did so, and had no trouble getting into the store. As they escaped, however, they were seen by a man who was passing by and he chased and captured them. Sidney showed considerable excitement in telling the story and appeared to realize the seriousness of what he had done.

It seemed clear that he was largely neglected by his parents and the question was raised whether this might not in part explain his behavior. For this reason his mother was urged to change her attitude, make him feel her interest in him and give him a feeling that she trusted rather than continually suspected him. His mother admitted that she had not paid much attention to him and realized that he needed both encouragement and affection.

The next step was to put him in another school. He very obviously wanted to get away from the close association with his sister. When told he was being put in another school, he said, "I'm glad I won't have to go with Ruth. I can look after myself. She's always bossed me. She's going to get a hard knock one of these times."

A few weeks later, he reported that everything was progressing well with him. He was delighted with the new school and described with much enthusiasm the building, laying stress on the gymnasium. When asked if he really liked it, he replied, "Yes, and I don't have Ruth hanging around." His teacher said he had done quite well with his studies, though there was decided room for improvement. He was looking forward to being made monitor at the swimming school and showed considerable pride at the prospect. When it was suggested to him that this would give him responsibility and that he would have to be careful not to abuse it, he replied, "Gee, I'll be fair to them. I know what that means."

Three weeks later his mother told the doctor she had noticed great improvement in his behavior, that he was more thoughtful and more patient. She attributed this to his talks with the doctor, but the latter pointed out that it was because of her willingness to show Sidney she expected good behavior and to praise him for it. She said that on New Year's Eve he had asked to go out with the other boys and she had at first said no, because he might get into mischief. Later, on thinking over what the doctor had said, she decided to let him go out and told him to be back early. This he did, which pleased her very much. The teacher at school also cooperated by making him a monitor of his class. Whatever the cause, there was a marked improvement in his school work, so that his report card showed B+ for effort, B for conduct and B for work. The next time he came to see the doctor, he reported that everything was pleasant at home, saying, "They all treat me all right now. I guess the trouble was with all of us." When asked how it was that he never got into trouble any more, he remarked, "I guess I'm having too good a time."

The record continued for another year. There were both ups and downs. He got into trouble in school once more, having come under the suspicion of stealing again. This was not proven and both his mother and teacher tried to show their continued confidence in him. Perhaps one factor in his progress was the changed attitude his mother took toward punishment. When his father wanted to whip him, she said to the doctor, "You know, I've come to believe as you do that a child should not be whipped or scolded all the time. He should be encouraged and helped to do better." When the record was closed, Sidney's attitude seemed fundamentally to have changed. He proudly related that now his parents and brothers and sisters trusted him all the time. He said he had no trouble with any of them. "Even Ruth has respect for me now."

George Costello

George was eleven years old when he was first sent to the doctor by his school teacher. She said he could do good work in every subject, but that he did not seem to be interested. He disturbed the class by shouting out, walking around the room, and hitting other pupils. He was insolent when asked to do something and usually replied, "I don't want to."

His father said that George was no problem at home and blamed the school system for his behavior in class. He felt that if they gave him a good whipping occasionally, he would behave himself. It was significant that both his brother and sister remarked that George was "scared to death" of his father. His mother did not whip him, but said she did scold him frequently. A former teacher said he had to be kept on the front seat and that neither kindness nor punishment were effective in controlling him. Pages might be written giving details of his misbehavior in class.

When he was asked the reason for his trouble in school, he unhesitatingly replied, "Oh, it's all my own fault. I was disobedient. I know I could make A if I tried. You see, I'm not bad at home, no sir. If I was, I'd get a good punishment from my father." Later he said, speaking of his parents, "My mother is best to me always and sometimes she does not tell my father on me. If she ever does, he slaps and kicks me and he sure can hurt." When the question of the school situation was raised, he said "Miss Smith, who is my teacher, is sometimes good to me. Sometimes when I raise my hand, she says, 'Put it down!', quick-like and that makes me mad. It's how she says it. Some of the fellows just holler the answers out. I do, too. I don't do it to tease her. It just pops out. I'm afraid she won't ask me. But if I holler the wrong answer, she says, 'There you are, always wrong when you holler,' but if I give the right answer, she just pays no attention to my answer, but asks someone who has not hollered it out. So what's the use of trying to suit her." When asked what he considered the real reason for his school misbehavior, he unhesitatingly replied, "Oh, it's just to show off. I don't do it at home, or anywhere else. If I did, I know it would only mean real trouble."

Although he spoke of liking the teacher, he gave the impression that in some way or other, he felt hurt. Finally, he told the following story: "She thinks I have some joke on her, I guess. When I buy her candy, she just throws it anywhere. I gave her a candy bell long ago and she just has it way up on a shelf in the closet. I saw it there, but I couldn't reach it or I would do as I did with some other candy I gave her that she just threw on her desk. I would take it and throw it away. Everybody else who buys her candy, she takes it quickly and says, 'So nice.' She never wants mine. She just throws mine aside and never eats it. She eats the other with her lunch. A while ago she had a party at school in her room. She sent me into the principal's room until after the party. She came in and brought the principal some cake and ice cream and went out. He said to me, 'I don't want it, George. Go ahead and eat it.' But I didn't want it either and I said, 'No,' and I did not eat it. After the party was all over, Miss Smith came to me and said, 'You can come up and have as much as you want of what is left.' But I wouldn't go. I was the only one she put out of the room. She thought I would be bad. How does she know? I didn't want the cake and ice cream unless I was at her party."

When asked what he considered was the cause of this treatment he received from his teacher, he said, "She doesn't like me." After a short period of quiet and apparent reflection, he remarked, "Well, I knew she didn't like me when I first went to her room, but she is sometimes good to me and I feel better. When I'm with the principal, I don't have any behavior, and one time another teacher came and took Miss Smith's place for a time and I got A in conduct."

When asked how that happened, he answered, "Well, I guess she didn't know I'd ever been bad in school."

Miss Smith's story was naturally somewhat different. She frankly considered him a pest. She said that when he paid attention, he learned his lessons quickly and well, but that this did not happen very often. He constantly tried to get the center of the stage. She considered him intelligent, but very queer. He came out with precocious and mature observations occasionally. When the life of Lincoln was read to the class, the story ended with the phrase, "And so Lincoln's soul passed to heaven and he was at rest." George objected to this, saying that nobody knew this definitely. He said that it might not be true at all.

A good deal of time was spent studying the situation at home. It became apparent that he received more punishment than he did affection. Speaking of his older brother, he said at one time, "Father said to Tom, 'Go ahead and beat him,' meaning me." He added he would rather have Tom beat him than his father, because the former used only his hands, while the latter used a strap. He then told of another time when his father had instructed Tom to give him a beating "anytime that he was bad," and, George continued, "He sure did."

The doctor discussed with the parents the boy's need for affection and confidence, and also pointed out to the teacher the same fact. This seemed to bring results and the next month none of his marks were below B, including the one for conduct. The doctor praised him for his, and added that he was sure he could get even higher marks. George said his teacher had been sending him on errands a lot lately, which he liked. The doctor explained to him that this was an indication of Miss Smith's appreciation of his good work and the realization that he could spare time from his studies.

His troubles were by no means all over. Some months later, he got on his teacher's nerves badly and she made him stay out of school for a day. Apparently she had told all the children to take their books home as she would confiscate any books found in their desks after class. George neglected to take his books and so she took them. The next day the class was doing English lessons and she inquired of George why he was idle. He retorted, "You have my book," which she thought was insolent. Later, he said the same thing about a pencil which he had left at home. This she thought very insolent and so she took the drastic step which has been mentioned. George came to see the doctor, sobbing and obviously greatly hurt. Finally, he burst forth with his side of the story, telling the same facts, only greatly colored by a conviction that Miss Smith was trying to pick on him. The doctor showed him how unfair this was, and how natural it was for Miss Smith to be annoyed with him when he answered her back as he did. He promised not to do so any more, since he wanted to keep in her good graces.

Some weeks later, speaking of her, he said, "She is better to me now. Today she let me make her lunch and mail her letters." He was greatly pleased with this attention and continued, "She had me erase the board and do everything for her." And then with a broad grin, he added, "I guess she likes me. I asked her to let me change my seat and you know she said, 'All right,' so I'm going to try and get As this month."

It was significant that his problems did not reappear until he got a new teacher who did not understand him or his needs. When the doctor asked why he had made trouble for this new teacher, he said, "Oh, I just wanted to be smart." After the doctor had explained the difference between real smartness and childish behavior, George remarked, "I guess I was just trying to be a little child." That seemed to be his last difficulty. A year later, his mother said he gave little trouble at home and his teacher said, "Don't worry about that boy. He is able to take care of himself."

WALTER KING

Walter King was the youngest child studied among the group of problem children. He was only four when he was referred by the superintendent of a day nursery as a child who made the lives of both workers and children miserable because of his unmanageableness. He was restless, untruthful, demanded constant attention and always insisted on being in the limelight. Whenever he was denied his own will, he had a tantrum in which he kicked off his shoes, threw them around, yelled and screamed.

In investigating the family situation, it was found that his father was a teamster accustomed to out-of-door work. The past year, however, he had been without regular employment, and was drinking heavily. He suffered from hernia and was afraid to undergo an operation.

His mother had started working in a factory when she was thirteen years of age. When she was nineteen she married, and continued to help out on the family income. For the past four or five years she had worked as a cleaning woman or a waitress.

Her attitude toward the head of the day nursery where Walter was having his trouble was very antagonistic. She did not believe what they told her of Walter's misbehavior and refused to coöperate with them in their treatment of him. She scoffed at the nursery's methods, and sometimes when she came for him in the evening she said jeeringly, "Come on, Walter, let me win you by love."

The father and mother had got along fairly well together until recently. Two weeks previously, however, he misconstrued a remark of hers, thinking she was insulting him by intimating that she was the bread winner when he ought to be. He became enraged and attacked her, giving her a black eye and almost choking her. She believed he would have killed her if she had not been able to fight him off. She had not heard from him since that time but had heard indirectly that he was taking treatment at Bellevue Hospital.

Walter's teacher reported that he was the most difficult child they had. They said he was selfish and self-assertive and always wanted the other children's toys. He insisted on having his own way and if denied it, would have a fearful tantrum. The other children had been much terrified by him. He would run up to them suddenly and snatch their toys out of their hands. One day in the dining room he became angry and knocked down two rows of chairs, swept off the table cloth, and pulled the curtains down. His teachers had tried to cure him by paying no attention to him but that did not work. They then tried to give him the responsibility of helping serve in the dining room. This worked for a short time, and he seemed to enjoy it. There was no doubt that Walter liked the limelight. Whenever a visitor came to the school, he was the first to rush to the teacher and try to attract the visitor's attention.

It was found that he had recently visited an aunt in New

Jersey and that his behavior had been particularly annoying since his return. This seemed, however, to be more of a protest against his return home than the result of unwise handling by his aunt. Since the child seemed to be so much better, as well as happier, with his aunt, the doctor suggested to his mother that she let him go there to live, but the latter would not permit it.

The following procedure was decided upon as a tentative method of solving Walter's troubles. First, effort was made to change his mother's present method of discipline so that the children would be relieved of the beatings which had been so frequent. Second, an attempt was made to change her feeling of antagonism toward the nursery. Third, the father's condition was to be dealt with with special reference to getting him a position, arranging for an operation for his hernia, and dealing, if possible, with his growing drunkenness.

Since it was believed that Walter's troubles depended so largely upon a solution of the father's difficulties, the first attack was made at that point. Mrs. King said that her husband used to be too strict with Walter. She said that he could not stand the noise, and trying to make the children keep still meant almost constant punishment. This had been greatly aggravated since Mr. King had become ill and lost his position. He never used to drink heavily until a year ago, but was now at it most of the time. She thought that might be due to his lack of employment, and realized that it was more difficult for him to get a position because of his hernia. She asked the doctor to see what he could do to arrange for an operation for him, and to persuade Mr. King of the necessity of having it done.

It was some time before Mr. King could be found as he was drinking steadily, and spent most of his time away from home. The doctor finally got in touch with him, however, and took up with him first the question of his hernia, asking if he realized how serious it was. Mr. King nodded silently and listened intently while the doctor explained the difficulty. He agreed that an operation was the best thing, that it would be the only way he could ever get a steady job again. Arrangements were made, therefore, for him to go to a hospital the following week. The operation was successfully performed at that time.

As soon as he had recovered from the operation, he was helped to find a position. Apparently the diagnosis as to the bearing of his illness and unemployment on his drunkenness was correct, as his drinking ceased to be a serious problem after he got regular employment.

Attention was then turned to Mrs. King. It was found that she was very unhappy in her job, due to continual supervision. While the worker from the bureau was discussing the problem with her, she found Mrs. King very much discouraged, and an investigator spent an afternoon with the woman who was employing her, telling her something about the family difficulty and asking if it were possible to deal with her in a more friendly fashion. Her employer responded cordially to the suggestion, and remarked that she had noticed how starved Mrs. King seemed to be for affection, and how much she seemed willing to do for someone who noticed her.

The next member of the family requiring attention was Walter's sister, Mildred. It was noticed that Walter played better and had fewer tantrums when his sister was not there.

When Mildred was in the group, it is true that she was able to quiet him at times, and enjoyed great influence over him, but she was extremely impudent and caused much trouble. Apparently Walter imitated her with delight. For that reason she was put in another class where she could not be a destructive example to him.

This indirect method of dealing with Walter's problems through attention to his family seemed to have had an effect. His teachers said that his tantrums had virtually ceased. He had, however, unfortunately developed new habits of biting and kicking other children, and he steadily refused to do what his teachers required. He seemed always to need to be in the center of the stage. His teacher admitted that he had improved when she paid a great deal of attention to him, allowing him to run errands, and praising him when he behaved, but she had come to the conclusion that this was not good for any child, and certainly was not fair to the other children to give Walter so much attention. The doctor tried to point out that perhaps the other children got their satisfactions in other ways in which Walter was deprived. Mrs. King's employer finally suggested that Walter be taken from school, and be allowed to stay with his mother during the afternoon. The employer herself gave him some attention, which not only pleased the child, but gave his mother great pleasure. The situation in the home cleared up largely because the father was regularly employed and in a healthier frame of mind, while Mrs. King was happier due to pleasant conditions of work. A report, made fourteen months after Walter was first brought to the doctor, indicated that he was making a good adjustment both to his home and to his new school, and Mrs. King reported that their home was happier than it had been for a long time. She said that everything was going well since Mr. King was employed regularly. Walter continued to be happy in his school and she said he was even bringing home good conduct records regularly.

HAROLD OSGOOD

Harold Osgood was nine years old when he was first brought to the office by his mother. She said that for about a year he had been extremely difficult to manage, had accomplished nothing in school and lied and stole. His parents had tried many ways of dealing with him, but none had been successful. He was considered the worst child in the family and was made most conscious of his shortcomings by reference to them, not only on the part of his parents, but by his sisters. Mr. and Mrs. Osgood had tried all kinds of punishment. Mr. Osgood had frequently whipped him with a belt, but without success. He had tried reasoning with him and depriving him of things, all to no effect. The week before Harold had been brought to the doctor, his teacher had punished him by having him remain in the room while the class went downstairs. When she returned, she missed some thumb tacks and pencils from her drawer. She asked Harold if anyone had been in the room and he answered no and also denied having taken the things himself. His teacher, however, looked in his school bag and found them there. She sent for his mother, who told him that God would certainly punish him for his action, which seemed to frighten the boy for a time.

It was apparent that Mrs. Osgood had no control over Harold. He irritated her thoroughly and made her nervous and excited. She said that within a year he had attempted to set fire to a house, had stolen money which had been laid aside for an insurance collector, and seemed in every way to have got beyond her control.

The first step was to give him a thorough physical examination and glandular medicine was prescribed. His school situation was investigated and it was decided to have him put in a special class where he could receive more individual attention. Although there were still times when he was incorrigible, his teacher seemed to feel that the added attention she was able to give him was helping him.

He had always played primarily with his sisters, and as he got older there had been little genuine recreation. He told the doctor he was tired of playing with his sisters and liked boys better than girls, since they were rougher. His parents were encouraged to give him more time for play and arrangements were made for him to join a Boy Scout troop. This seemed to meet his need for feeling masculine.

The basic problem, however, in solving Harold's difficulties proved to be the general situation in the family. Their economic condition was acute. Mrs. Osgood earned about $7.00 a week. Mr. Osgood had been ill, but was at that time making $20.00 a week. There had been times when the family would have had to go without food, had it not been for a small supply of canned goods which was in the house. They had had a boarder who had paid them $5.00 a week, but she had now left. About two years earlier, Mr. Osgood had been seized with epilepsy. Several times he had fallen and hurt himself and it had grown increasingly difficult for him to hold any position.

Mrs. Osgood herself was in very poor health, due in part,

at least, to the need for a set of false teeth. The combination of financial worry and ill health made it quite impossible for the parents to deal adequately with Harold's problems, and so attention had to be directed to the general family difficulties. Mr. Osgood was sent to a clinic and medicine was provided. A set of teeth was procured for Mrs. Osgood. A house was found for them where they would be comfortable but would not have as high a rent, and a charitable institution arranged to contribute a certain amount of money until the family could get on its feet. After this was done and they were all in a less worried state of mind, they were again approached and Harold's problems discussed with them. They were urged not to treat the boy as though he were a special problem and not to speak of his faults in his presence. It was suggested that he receive less nagging and more affection.

Six months later, his teacher said that she had noticed a decided change for the better, both in his physical condition and in his behavior. His marks had been B, B+, and A, and there had been no more serious charges against him than occasional talkativeness. The case was considered a genuine success.

FRANK HOLT

Frank Holt's case was of a very different type than was usually referred to the doctors. He was a boy fifteen years old who had failed in school. His mother was deeply concerned over this failure and threatened suicide when she heard he was not to be promoted. His conduct had always been satisfactory and he had never been a problem in school, except for this failure. His parents had come to this country after they had grown up; they had always worked desperately hard and had never had the opportunity for an education. Frank was their only son and they had pinned all their hopes on him. He was to be the success which they had never been. His mother dramatically described receiving a note from the school principal, from which she learned that he was not to be promoted. She got it out of the mail box and carried it to Frank. He read it and she noted his face grow white. Finally he told her what the trouble was. She said they must both die if he failed and threatened to jump out of the window.

Frank was a tall, attractive boy, who was friendly and polite. His manly appearance, however, was completely off-set by his reliance on the coaxing and prodding of whatever adult he happened to be with. He gave up easily in the face of difficulty, and seemed to lack completely any capacity for foresight and independence. Upon investigation, it was found that he had never been given any real responsibility. He had recently been hunting a job and had been offered the position of playing in an orchestra, but his mother broke the contract he had signed. The doctor explained to her that Frank depended too much on others and that she should encourage him and throw him more upon his own resources. She realized this and wanted him to be a man. But she said that if he were not frequently reprimanded, he would do nothing. She thought if he were left alone in the evening, he would not study, but would only waste his time. She also said his music teacher had frequently asked him to practice more, but that if she were not at home, he would not do it. She wanted him to continue with his lessons. The doctor pointed out that this was an opportunity to make him rely upon himself and that if he wished to continue his lessons, the responsibility for practicing must rest upon himself. Another way in which his mother dominated him was in regard to his plans for a future career. She had decided he must become a lawyer, since she had a nephew who had done well in that profession. The boy himself admitted he had no wish whatsoever to become a lawyer, but he had acquiesced to her wishes.

His father took much the same attitude as his mother, feeling that Frank must be continually supervised since he was unable to accept responsibility. He also felt that Frank was lazy and that if he were not continually scolded, he would neither study nor practice. His idea of the proper method of meeting the situation was to scold the boy constantly. When it was suggested that they put responsibility upon him, both parents were very dubious of the results. Frank told the doctor he would be much more interested in practicing if he had another instrument than the violin, preferably a saxophone. He said the kind he wanted could be purchased in small monthly payments and he could see no reason why his mother would not consent. It was obvious that he had had no experience in money affairs, since when he needed money for necessary things, his parents gave it to him. He seemed pleased with the suggestion that he be put on an allowance, so that if he wanted extras, he could get them if he wanted them badly enough to give up other things. He was puzzled to know how he would know ahead of time what his expenses would be, but he was interested in working out a plan.

His greatest difficulty in school had been with mathematics. He seemed to have no conception whatever even of arithmetic. When the doctor asked him in the spring what he was going to do about it, he said he thought that in September he would be able to work hard enough to catch up. The doctor pointed out that would obviously be impossible and suggested he make arrangements to do that work during the summer. Frank accepted the suggestion and found a friend who was willing to tutor him. He reported to the doctor during the summer and was able to show marked improvement. Once during the latter part of the summer when he called at the office, he was neatly dressed in a new suit, which was the first clothing he had ever earned for himself. He had hunted up a job and had worked at it most of the summer. He had also purchased his saxophone and was paying monthly installments on it. His mother gave him a dollar a day for carfare and lunch and he saved from that for his payments. His mother was still having a great deal of difficulty letting him have any independence. He had had a chance to play in a band and earn $65.00 a week, but she turned it down. The doctor discussed this with her later and she recognized the truth of his position, saying, "I understand that Frank is now getting to be a man." She said she did not nag him as much about his school work and added with pride that he was doing better with his music.

She was still very much discouraged about his future and seemed to recognize that the law was out of the question as a profession for him. As she said, "Frank will not work hard, for he is lazy." That seemed to be the attitude of everyone, that it was entirely his fault for not studying and working harder. It was pointed out that the trouble might partly lie in the fact that he had not found his right niche, and that nothing which had been suggested really appealed to him. There could be no development of responsibility so long as he was entirely concerned with issues which had been chosen for him by his parents rather than those which he chose for himself.

Three months later Frank said things were going better at school, but that there was not much change at home. He got little definite satisfaction from his mother about anything in which he was interested. He said he had spoken to her several times about taking up music as a profession, but had never been able to get any answer from her. He spoke with considerable feeling in telling these things about his mother, but he smiled as he added, "My father is willing I should do anything, and he is always trying to encourage me along." When the doctor asked him, "Suppose you only had yourself to think about, no parents, no doctor, in fact, no one to try to influence you in any way in your choice of life work, what do you think you would do?" Without hesitation, Frank answered, "Well, if that could be, I would go right into music. That is really what I want to do." He then said he had been made leader of his band and that he was planning to hold regular practice and go out for engagements to play. During the summer he hoped to find some place where his band could play for the entire season. In the course of the conversation, he spoke several times almost resentfully of his mother's attitude toward his ambition, but whenever he spoke of his father, he smiled cheerfully and at one time said, "Father says, 'Go to it,' and I'm going to do it."

A month later he spoke of a new orchestra which had been organized. He said they had established regular practice periods and thus far had been prompt and enthusiastic. He also said his mother was now much more agreeable and was showing interest in his new endeavor. Before leaving, he said he had decided to go into music permanently, but added, "I've not given up all intention of getting further education, but I hope to arrange things so that I can take some studies at night school."

Some months later, he said he was now working steadily and was planning to purchase a new and expensive saxophone. The doctor went closely into the matter in an endeavor to test the strength of his plan, to show him how one should carefully estimate one's chances before going ahead. Frank seemed to realize that this was a real adventure and that he stood to win or lose on his own merits, without expecting any assistance from his family in case he could not meet the payments. The doctor encouraged him and showed him that his success would be a fine proof of his ability to achieve, both to himself and to his family.

At his last visit to the doctor, Frank said everything was going splendidly at school. He said he was getting all the music he needed and that his other studies were going satisfactorily. He also said his mother's attitude had changed entirely. She was then quite willing for him to take summer work in an orchestra outside the city and it was clear that he was both willing and able to accept responsibility.

Goodwin Carey

If ever there was a problem child, it was Goodwin Carey. When, as a boy of fourteen, he was referred to the doctor, he had the reputation of being both sullen and bad tempered. He refused to do his class work and mocked his teacher and seemed altogether incorrigible.

His father believed in strict discipline and said that when you talked to a boy he forgot, but when you whipped him he remembered. His mother had been called to the school the day before he was referred. She was thoroughly exasperated and humiliated and created quite a scene in school. She slapped Goodwin, wished that he would catch cold and die, get run over by an automobile, and said he was ruining the entire family. His teachers said that he did not play well with the other boys because of his domineering attitude. He always wanted to boss everything and fight. One teacher said that he had the hardest face of any child she had ever seen. His own story was that his latest difficulty was the result of his calling out very loudly to his teacher, "Good morning, Miss." She told him to go right downstairs. He did not obey, and after that they put him back two grades. He added, "I wouldn't mind if they had scolded or punished me in some other way, but to put me back two grades, I don't think was fair."

His mother was very anxious to have the boy put under the doctor's care, but said that it was difficult to get him to come. The doctor persuaded her not to try to bring him herself, but to have him come alone, as it would make him feel more independent and grown up. The doctor explained the conflict each child meets during adolescence of wanting to remain infantile and of also wanting to be considered grown up. He pointed out that Goodwin needed less supervision and more independence.

It was decided that his mother was to give him more responsibilities, and encourage him to accept them as far as possible. Second, that his father should be urged to take more interest in the boy. Third, his teachers were to give him more responsibility, that he might have the feeling of achievement. Both his mother and his teachers seemed willing and able to coöperate.

The boy was sent to a camp during the summer and had

a wonderful time. He amused the family after his return by recounting his experiences. He had been especially impressed by the story of a camp leader whom Goodwin said had once been "a bum and had made the struggle and won out." That fall he was encouraged to follow out his interest in boxing and wrestling. Physically he was smaller for his age than most boys, and it seemed clear that he needed decidedly to gain satisfaction along this line.

That fall things went along well in school for some time. Finally, however, there was a flare-up over a trivial incident. The doctor induced Goodwin to talk as freely as possible of this latest difficulty and discussed with him his side of the question and his part in the affair. He pointed out to him that his idea of a grudge on the teacher's part possibly originated in his own relationship and feelings toward her. Goodwin seemed fair-minded and said, "You see I am this way, if I think a person doesn't like me or has a grudge against me, I just accept it and I feel they would never change no matter what I did." The doctor then suggested that as he was so quickly entering the manhood stage as indicated by his physical development and interest in sports, it would be well for him also to try and develop a more manly attitude towards school affairs and assume more responsibility for success in behavior as well as studies. He pointed out frankly that much of Goodwin's trouble was due to the fact that he was still meeting many small unimportant situations in the same manner that he did as a child. To this Goodwin quickly responded by saying, "Well, I guess I have, but a fellow can't change over all of a sudden, can he?" The doctor suggested that frequently boys of his intelligence and interest did make rapid transformations and Goodwin agreed to try to think over that viewpoint.

That winter his mother said it was remarkable how much he had improved. His trouble at school had blown over. He was wearing long trousers, kept his clothes clean, and brushed his hair. She also said that he waited on her and was very considerate of her welfare. She smiled with considerable satisfaction as she related these changes. His principal also said that there had been marked improvement. The doctor stressed the fact that the confidence they had shown in the boy had been responsible for these results.

When the case was closed the teacher said that it had been his best term in school and that he was giving no trouble at all. His mother said that she felt that one of the principal reasons for success was the fact that both she and the older boys had been treating him in a more grown-up way. In the last school difficulty she had let him feel he had her backing but had put it up to him to find the solution.

Edward Perry

Edward Perry was eleven years old when he was referred by his teacher, who felt that he was not unintelligent and could do his work, but was inattentive and accomplished little. He was then in 3B for the third time. When his mother was interviewed, she did not show any special affection for him and was evidently little concerned about him. She constantly spoke with much emotion of her favorite son, who had recently died.

She said she had never been happy with her husband. They were married when she was only seventeen and he was twenty-four. She hardly knew him at all before they were married and would never have consented if her mother had not forced her.

Mr. Perry seemed not to care much about any of the children except his youngest daughter. He played with her, mended her toys, and caressed her a great deal. He paid little attention to Edward, but scolded or hit him at times if he did something he did not like.

In school, Edward was considered a nuisance because he tried so persistently to get the attention of the other children. This, however, was the only specific example of bad conduct which was given. He apparently got along well with the other children.

On his first visit to the doctor, Edward spoke of Bill, a boy whom he greatly admired. Describing Bill's conduct in class, he said, "He yells and talks right out. He's the worst boy in class and I'm next." The doctor asked him how it was he was not the worst. He smiled and said, "There can't be no worse than he is." He was asked who the best boy was, to which be unhesitatingly replied, "Thomas is the best. He's nothing but a little sissy. He's the kind that doesn't want to play with anyone. He's afraid to do what others do. He's afraid to go down in my underground hut." He tried to account further for Thomas' reputation by saying, "He never talks in school. He never yells out any time. He always waits for the teacher and he always raises his hand."

The doctor explained to Edward that he did not want him to be a sissy, but that neither did he want him to be a tough. He drew a diagram and made a line with Thomas at one end and Bill at the other and near the middle made a branching line to indicate the road to real manhood, explaining to him as far as he could why Thomas acted as a sissy and why Bill, on the other hand, still retained much of his babyhood behavior. When Edward was asked which road he wanted to go, he at once said, "I want to go up here and be a man."

The doctor then added a further explanation as to the difference between these extremes in the attitude and behavior of a real manly boy. As he started to go, Edward picked up the piece of paper, put it in his pocket and said, "I'm going to keep that. That's what I'd like to be," but added, "I don't see how you can be if you have to go to a teacher like I have." The doctor then spent a little more time endeavoring to show the boy that even with that teacher he could alter his behavior, and he finally replied, "Well, I guess I'll stay in there for a while."

Edward had an older brother, Stephen, with whom he quarreled continually, but it seemed that this brother could help decidedly in solving Edward's difficulties, and so the doctor had a conference with him. Stephen admitted that they had not got along well, but said that he would like to help his brother. It was arranged that Edward should help him with his paper route and be paid for it. This would give Stephen a chance to exercise some supervision and also give Edward the satisfaction of being partially independent.

It was some time later that Edward came to the doctor's office to tell him that he was more "grown up" than before and that he was behaving better in school. Only once in a while did he walk around the classroom without permission. Referring to the previous discussion, the doctor asked him what he thought it meant to be grown up and Edward replied that he thought it meant to be manly and have good manners. The doctor suggested that perhaps good judgment entered into it as well, that when he came by himself to see the doctor he would have to use judgment in asking directions and then following them, and that if he could not do this, he would not be grown up enough to come by himself.

Edward felt sure he was grown up enough for this and the doctor then pointed out that he probably was, but that he did not seem to be grown up while he was in the school-room. The boy seemed to get the point.

There was need for continual encouragement if Edward were to take any steps ahead. He wanted to join the Scouts, but was discouraged at the number of things he had to learn. He kept repeating that he was unable to do this. But when the doctor helped him, he found to his great surprise that within a half hour, he had memorized perfectly the first seven tests and had learned to tie the first four knots, in spite of his protests that "I can't learn that." He frequently did say, "Now let me try it all by myself," showing his ambition to learn. He was easily discouraged but equally easily encouraged when spoken to kindly. Before leaving, he asked if he might be allowed to return the following week, saying, "I want you to see how I remember these we did, and have you teach me some more."

When contact was lost with the family, it seemed that Edward was on the road to adjustment. His parents had moved into a new home where they were happier and where the boy was able to make better friends. His mother made a definite effort to understand the doctor's attitude and came to speak of Edward as a nervous child rather than as a nuisance. Hers was far from being an ideal attitude, but it was an improvement and Edward was having more satisfying relations with her. Although the father expressed an interest in Edward's problem, he did not comprehend enough of it to see where he could be useful in the treatment. The school situation was favorable. Principal and teacher were interested, and although they considered Edward a problem, they tried to interest him and work with him. Apparently, most important of all was the understanding which he came to have of his own behavior. He very definitely took as a goal the ideal of growing up. This ideal seemed vague, but the doctor filled it with positive content which the boy was able to grasp.

Albert Hunt

Albert Hunt was sixteen years of age when he was referred to the doctor because of having run away from home several times. During the recent holidays, he had disappeared for two days and nights. His mother discovered finally that he was sleeping in an empty room in a near-by apartment. The trouble had arisen when he had brought home $7.50, which he had earned, and she had refused to give him back any of it for himself. When he threatened to leave, his mother told him to take off the good clothes she had paid for and to wear his old ones. He did so and went out. Later she found the following note in the letter box, "Mrs. Hunt: I would like to have the $7.50 which you promised me and also allow me to have my clothes, which I am sure you cannot use, but I can. Thanking you in advance for your trouble, I am, Yours, A. Hunt." Two days later his mother met him on the corner and told him to come home as he could not have had anything to eat and his being away was spoiling her holiday. When he came in, his brother Raymond told Albert to apologize to his mother, and when he refused, hit him violently. Albert finally went to his mother, saying he was only apologizing because be was forced to and not because he wanted to.

In investigating his school record, it was found that his grades varied from just barely passing in English and Spanish to bad failures in French, geometry and chemistry. There was no record, however, that he had ever been a conduct problem at school.

In discussing the problem, Albert said that his brother had always tried to boss him. The doctor talked over with him the possible origin of this behavior on the part of Raymond, showing him the earlier childhood relationships and went into the question of family jealousies. Albert showed rather an unusual insight in understanding the mechanisms that might lie behind his brother's present reactions toward the family. He spoke of his sister four years younger than himself and smilingly remarked, "Now I remember thinking mother always did consider her the baby and pet. I guess that was just my jealousy." Further on he said, "That time I left home and stayed away must have been due to all this, too." He then recalled several recent difficulties which he seemed delighted to analyze for himself. Before going he said, "When one looks at these things, one sees them in a different light, but they sure did cause a lot of hard feeling at the time. I guess I was in a rather bad place in the family, but, perhaps, the trouble was in myself."

The next time Albert came to the doctor's office, he seemed contented and happy. When he was a child, his nose had been broken and as a result his appearance had been unattractive. He was sensitive about this and so arrangements had been made for an operation, which had taken place. There had been an immediate reaction in the way of added pride in his appearance. He proudly displayed his school card, saying he had passed all his subjects, adding that he did this because

"I wanted to show you I could do it, but I was afraid I would have to carry one subject over to next term. I guess it was the reviewing got me over."

He was much cut up, however, over the way his brother was still treating him. He told of a quarrel at home which had arisen because he had asked his mother if he could have a new suit of clothes. She had promised that he could, but later spoke to his brother about it. Raymond opposed the idea, although he knew that Albert needed the clothes as he was to graduate from school in June. The class was having a theater night and a class night before that time and Albert was anxious to attend these functions. Raymond had said, however, "Let him get out and earn the clothes if he wants some." Albert was feeling very sore against both his brother and mother, claiming that the former had beaten him during the argument. He said that he could not stand such treatment, especially as his mother had changed her mind to agree with his brother. He was ready to leave home permanently and start work, but the doctor had a long visit with him about the trouble and the boy promised to remain at home, at least for the time being.

He came in a month later to report that he was doing well at school, better, he thought, than ever before. When asked how he and Raymond were getting along, he said they had not quarreled since he had seen the doctor last "for the simple reason that we have not spoken since." He felt the present relationship was a rest for them all, for if one should speak to the other, there would at once be an argument. The doctor inquired if as young men they could not talk of impersonal things, but Albert felt sure that if he started the conversation, Raymond would accept it as a weakness on his part "and take advantage of it to bawl me out." The doctor tried to show him that as young men they should be able to settle their difficulties on a different basis and Albert remarked, "Yes, I know we ought, but he doesn't see it in that light."

To the doctor's surprise, not many days later this elder brother came of his own accord to see him. He introduced himself by saying, "I am Albert's brother. He has talked to me of you and I thought I would come in and see you." He appeared to be interested in Albert, but had little insight at first into the boy's difficulties and peculiar home relationships. The doctor passed over the main features in the case, explaining some of the mechanisms as he saw them. Raymond was greatly interested and said that such an approach had never occurred to him. He not only asked intelligent questions, but recalled occasions in the home life and many events in his own personal life and seemed to enjoy applying his new-found knowledge to explaining difficulties. He spoke of his mother and said he felt quite confident that little could be done directly to show her things in this light, but he offered to influence her to "lay off the kid" and said he also would treat Albert differently, especially letting him feel more independent. He thought it would be well to let Albert carry out his plan of going to camp that summer as that would make him feel that his wishes had gained some recognition. Raymond was so enthusiastic over the doctor's approach to Albert's problems that he asked permission to come in some day and talk over some of his own difficulties.

Late that spring, Albert came in to see the doctor again. He spoke with obvious pleasure of his coming graduation from school and remarked, "I did even better than I expected to." He spoke of his prospects and ambitions and the marked change in the home relationships, saying, "I think your talk helped Raymond to understand things better, for he has been entirely different at home ever since, and seems anxious now to help me, where before he seemed delighted to oppose me," and then added, "I guess we all understand things better."

PART THREE

AN EVALUATION OF ETHICAL THEORIES IN THE LIGHT OF THE EMPIRICAL DATA

Chapter I

THE PLACE OF PUNISHMENT IN THE DEVELOPMENT OF RESPONSIBILITY

Any empirical study of situations where punishment has been used raises the question as to its effectiveness. Has it accomplished its purpose? It is clear that there are two angles from which a study can be made. Does the punishment in a specific situation deter others from committing a similar act, and does it reform the individual concerned so that he will act differently in the future? Obviously the first question is sadly in need of evidence. This particular study, however, is primarily concerned with the individual punished. What punishments are effective for reformation, and under what circumstances should they be applied?

In analyzing the cases recorded in order to discover where punishment has been ineffective or even dangerous, one notes at once times when it has been used capriciously, or where a course of action has been weakly abandoned. One of the most interesting illustrations of the danger implicit in this latter attitude was to be seen in the story of Hugh Carr. When the doctor persisted in his examination in spite of the boy's protests, Hugh was refreshingly frank as to why he had made such a noise. "That's the way I do." It was the way which had always worked. Here was a new situation; whining and shrieking did not work, and the lad had only respect and affection for the doctor who had firmly insisted on necessary obedience. It is apparent that where there was a lack of persistence on the part of the parents, not only was there no real punishment, but also the child was helped to form the belief that, when he got into an unpleasant situation as a result of his own acts, he could get out of it by whines and cries.

Another case brought out this danger even more clearly. Walter King, though he was only four years old, had a record for unmanageableness worthy of one three times his age. His mother had almost completely lost control over him. When he was crossed "he had tantrums in which he lay on the floor and screamed," and he was quite willing, if necessary, to throw his shoes around and wreck the furniture. This happened when his mother was trying to discipline him, but, curiously enough, it was found that his father could exact obedience with a quiet word. There were many factors involved, but unquestionably one was that Walter knew his father made no idle threats, that he thoroughly meant what he said. He was equally sure his mother did not mean what she said, that she was in all probability bluffing. At least it was worth a tantrum or two to find out.

Another type of ineffective punishment was that in which the reason for it, or its justice, was not clearly understood. Too often was it assumed unjustifiably that the child was aware of just what act had called forth the punishment, or why a particular act should merit it. The punishment was administered without an adequate attempt to point out the implications of the act in question. The result was either resentment or bewilderment. So far, these criticisms are practical details and do not affect seriously the conventional theory of punishment; but we now turn to more fundamental considerations.

One of the most serious problems raised in any consideration of punishment is the resentment which so often follows. Where this happens the punishment is obviously less effective, or even dangerous. In the cases studied this seemed to be a problem of age, in part at least. The younger the child the less likelihood there was of personal antagonism resulting, while, on the other hand, the older the child the greater was the danger of resentment being the only outcome of the punishment. A more important cause of this antagonism, however, was anger on the part of the one doing the punishing.

There was no doubt that Allen Hobart deliberately tormented his mother. He seemed to invite punishment, rather than dread it. "He gets a real kick out of being devilish," and the more punishment there was, the more deviltry he showed. It was a thoroughly vicious circle. If Allen, however, got a "kick" out of his misbehavior, it seemed equally clear that his mother got a "kick" out of punishing him. Punishment for her was in no sense a carefully calculated instrument to be used only with an eye to its effectiveness. When she pounded her child until someone had to pull her off, she was having an emotional debauch. Her feelings of resentment demanded some powerful outlet. The child sensed that fact. He apparently realized that he was being punished less for his own benefit than for her satisfaction. His punishment was an outlet for her uncontrolled emotions. Her anger bred in him a similar feeling. It seemed possible, also, that Allen rather relished the sense of power which he got from realizing that he could throw his mother into such a fit of temper. The punishment was unpleasant to be sure, but after all it could be endured. Proudly he came to the place where he could say: "You can't hurt me." From then on he was master, perversely enjoying his mother's tantrums.

One is reminded of Westermarck's theory of the joys of resentment. There may be very legitimate doubt as to whether such feelings are as inevitable as he assumed, and even more question as to how fully they may be socialized, but that there is such a thing as positive enjoyment of resentment seems fully demonstrated. It is here that there is need for a careful analysis of the results of punishment. It was assumed by Bentham, and by many others after his time, that because punishment was obviously unpleasant it would, therefore, deter the offender from similar behavior in the future. What was not seen was the complexity of possible reactions. Instead of a lack of satisfaction there might be very genuine pleasure from the resentment which followed; instead of deterrent dissatisfaction there might be positive combative satisfaction. Where this was the case, not only was the punishment ineffective, but there were, at times, even more serious attitudes developed. Since this was the result, the question should be raised as to whether punishment does not defeat its own purpose when administered by one who is angry.

The cases of both Hugh and Allen illustrate another danger; that resulting from punishment not directed at some specific habit. Hugh's parents apparently did not realize that his actions might be understood in the light of a child groping more or less blindly after normal satisfactions. They did not believe there was any cause for his misbehavior. He was just mean; as such to be tolerated as long as possible, and then to be beaten. Had they grasped the fact that there were satisfactions at stake, they might have picked out a specific habit with which they were dissatisfied, and thus produced a specific dissatisfaction in him. Believing in his "meanness," however, they controlled themselves as long as possible, then punished him for everything that had happened since the last punishment. That could only result in *mutual* resentment and bewilderment.

One of the most frequent forms of punishment is that of social isolation of one kind or another, and the cases were analyzed to see under what situation it was effective. Goodwin Carey was fourteen years old when he was first brought to the doctor as a child who was disobedient, sullen, and bad tempered. He had been regarded as the black sheep of the family. Not only his parents, but also his brothers and sisters, were in the habit of speaking to others in his presence of his incorrigibility. He became completely unmanageable after his mother went to school one day, and slapped him in front of his classmates. From then on nothing mattered, because nothing worse could happen to him. There was a marked change, however, when the doctor expressed his liking for and belief in him, and even more when his family was persuaded to cease acting as though he were the family disgrace, and really take him into the family circle.

There is an unquestioned place for the kind of punishment which creates a feeling of social isolation. It has long been recognized that social pressure exercised in this way is a most powerful means of bringing a recalcitrant individual into line with the wishes of society. There has not, however, been an adequate realization of the grave dangers implicit in this attitude. No one, child or adult, will voluntarily remain in exile. If one social group is closed, another will be found before very long.

It was apparent in the cases studied that the effectiveness of this kind of punishment was lessened or altogether lost where the social isolation was long continued. When this happened the patient lost sight of the cause of the punishment, and, like Goodwin, concentrated on gaining some kind of social security, as well as on venting his wrath against the cause of his trouble. Among the cases studied there were many which illustrated this tendency to gain attention, a place in the social sun, by fair means or foul. Nothing mattered so long as the isolation were ended, and all too often the original cause of the trouble was forgotten by all parties concerned. In the case of Goodwin, his faults could not be touched until he was taken back into society, and given a sense of belonging. At that point something constructive could be accomplished.

The case of Harold Osgood illustrates an analogous situation. He was a nine-year-old boy who was not only disobedient, but had formed decided habits of lying and stealing. There were various factors involved, and treatment had to be directed toward the entire family situation. Obviously one of the first needs was to reëstablish the boy's confidence in himself. He had been criticized so steadily, and encouraged so little, that he had no faith in his capacity for accomplishing any reformation.

Society has seen that it is necessary at times to make the individual question the rightness of some attitude, to shake his confidence in the wisdom of some habit. Social isolation is an admirable instrument for accomplishing this result. When this is carried very far, however, it defeats its own purpose, for it cuts the nerve of effort. Unless there is membership in a social group there is little confidence, and without confidence, effort seems neither worth while nor possible. As far as a child is concerned, it is the confidence which comes from a warm sense of *family* support which is most important.

This conclusion may throw some light on the so-called "anti-social" individuals with whom society is so abundantly supplied. They are the ones whose behavior has been so obnoxious that they have been "ruled out" of society as the only means of dealing with them. But is this effective? If they are expelled from one group, will they not seek another? Here perhaps is the source in part of our gangs—outlawed groups who have as a common bond this social isolation. It is not implied that these individuals can be reformed simply by taking them back into the social groups which originally expelled them. But it is suggested that they will remain in their gangs where they have companionship and security until society finds some way of linking them up with more constructive groups. Here, too, permanent social isolation defeats its own purpose.

Both of these cases raise a prior question. Are there individuals who, because of a general lack of social security and personal confidence, should be treated with especial care? Do such people need punishment, or, to put it another way, is it possible to punish them? They feel that society is critical in any event, and become abnormally sensitive and build a wall of reserve around themselves. What is needed with such persons is not added criticism, which must necessarily only increase the problem, but a building up of social security and personal confidence. Only when that is accomplished can anything constructive be done in changing old patterns or in building new ones.

Another type of ineffective punishment is that administered by one who was not recognized as having authority or who was not respected. At eleven years of age William Simmons was a confirmed truant and an habitual thief. His problem proved to be a discouraging one, requiring long and patient handling. One of the factors which was discovered to be at the root of his trouble was the fact that responsibility for punishing him was cheerfully accepted by a large family of brothers and sisters, as well as by his parents. The result was not only complete uncertainty as to just who was going to punish and when, but also a deep-seated resentment against being ruled over by those who were more or less his contemporaries. He did not seem to resent the punishment which came from his father and mother, apparently recognizing that that was their parental privilege. His self respect, however, was fundamentally shaken by the continuous reproaches of those but little older than himself. His case could not be dealt with until this fraternal supervision was ended.

The evidence indicates that if punishment is to be effective it must be given by a person who is respected. There is evidence, also, which points to a similar conclusion regarding affection between punished and punisher. There is a frequent assumption, especially in theological circles, that punishment must be administered by one who is *loving*. A truer statement would seem to be that, if it is to be effective, it should be only at the hands of one who is *loved*.

The vexed question of corporal punishment had to be faced as a separate issue. Were there times when it was a successful instrument of reformation? Did it ever accomplish anything more than to provide an outlet for the outraged feelings of the one who performed the operation? No final answer can be given, of course. All that can be said is that in the fifty cases studied none was found where it seemed to be successful. That may have been because most of the children studied had come from homes where the punishment was abnormally severe. It might have been used more constructively in small quantities. Another possible reason is that most of the children were above the age of six, only one was as young as four. There seems little doubt that the age factor is very great at this point. The older the child, apparently the more apt physical punishment was to create personal resentment and blind fury, rather than dissatisfaction with the habit in question.

At best, however, corporal punishment seemed a dangerous instrument. Not only was it apt to arouse anger, there was also difficulty in persuading the victim that he had not been the unwilling vehicle for the satisfaction of another's emotional needs. Children seemed not to be unanimously convinced that there was any great amount of truth in the oft-repeated remark that "it hurts me more than it does you." They saw with astonishing clarity behind their parents' motives. "She gets mad, and so she beats me up."

There was no doubt that physical punishment had a thoroughly bad effect on Allen and Hugh. At a time when they should have been encouraged to grow up and adopt mature ways, they were treated in a manner which made them feel like little children, and reduced them to feelings of impotent rage. Had they been very young such punishment might have been effective, but even then the results would have had to be watched with the greatest care.

Mention has been made of the danger of punishment which

creates too strong a feeling of social isolation, or which in any way breaks down confidence. Physical punishment did this almost invariably. One of the two results seemed well-nigh universal. Sometimes the child's spirit was broken. More frequently, however, there was the opposite reaction. They toughened themselves to it, taking pride in their achievement. As Allen said: "You can't hurt me."

Robert Rignana was thirteen years of age when he was referred for truancy and bad conduct. He told the doctor his mother used a strap on him. He sometimes played at school until he was late for dinner, and she would hit him and send him to bed. At one time, after being severely whipped, he flippantly remarked: "I don't care, that's no good." He may not have been truthful in the first part of the statement, but he was manifestly right when he said that it was no good.

In *Changing Conceptions of School Discipline,* Harris tells the story of the place of corporal punishment in education. For long it was never questioned. "Spare the rod and spoil the child" was the ruling principle. Gradually educators became less sure, and its place was limited more and more. Other forms of discipline were found to be more effective and less dangerous, until finally it was ruled out entirely. With the shift in education from a day when obedience was the primary value to the more modern times when original-ity was more highly valued, mere coercion lost favor. Greater interest was had in punishments which would not destroy the child's self-respect and which would direct attention to the causes of the trouble.

When one sees punishment which results primarily in resentment because it is capricious or administered angrily, punishment which is ineffective because it touches symptoms rather than causes, punishment which has no other result than to break down confidence and create a sense of social isolation, when one sees all this there comes a realization that it is not as simple a matter to punish effectively as it was once thought.

Reference has been made to Bentham's view that it is easier to punish than it is to reward. He was thinking of it in the legal sense, but even here there is room for doubt. We are just beginning to evaluate legal punishment from the standpoint of what it accomplishes, and discovering that it is often ineffective because the psychological reactions on the part of criminals are similar to those which characterized the children in this study. Recent studies of criminology indicate that corporal penalties bring resentment against law, increased bravado, courage, and hatred, even as it does often with children.

The fact is that the psychological reactions are by no means as simple as men once thought. Bain's psychology was more adequate than Bentham's because he did recognize the habit basis. He saw that men did not need to be moved to action solely by love of pleasure or fear of pain. He did not see, however, how very complex our reactions are, and therefore could not realize how frequently punishment is ineffective, or even, at times the cause of perverse satisfaction.

It has not been difficult to discover illustrations of punishment which accomplished no constructive results. We are in a very much more difficult field when we try to evaluate the cases where punishment seems to have been effective.

Human activity is purposive, seeking satisfaction in some

form or other. This implies a causal sequence, first a desire or need followed by some means of satisfying it. Hence the only way we have to change and control human nature is by discovering the causes behind any action, finding out the need which lies at its heart, and then meeting it in a more satisfying manner. If this is true, how fully may punishment be used to accomplish this end?

The very word "punish" implies the desire to give not satisfaction but dissatisfaction. It is in other words fundamentally and inherently a negative instrument. Where habits have been built up which society finds unsatisfactory, punishment is the instrument for breaking down such habits. Wisely used, it can accomplish this result. It is, at times, a necessary preliminary to positive reconstruction of character.

Bearing these assumptions in mind the following may be given as a working definition of punishment. Punishment is any means which may be used to make a person dissatisfied with some existing habit. It is distinguished from praise or encouragement in that the means taken are unpleasant, either intrinsically or in their results.

One common assumption regarding punishment needs to be challenged. It is often thought that punishment is inevitably accompanied by some attitude of blame or resentment toward the one who is thought to have done wrong. That this is often true, cannot be questioned. But the results of this study sharply challenge the assumption that the attitude of blame is inevitable, and, in the second place, that the most effective punishment includes a feeling of anger or resentment. Punishment must not be an outlet for feelings of resentment if it is to be an instrument of control.

Donald Morio furnished the opportunity for an interesting

study of punishment effectively applied. He had been detected stealing in the office where he was employed. The record of the incident was fairly complete. His employer had not wanted to have the boy punished, believing that he gave good promise of later development, and would respond to kindness. At first Donald agreed to repay what had been taken, but that proved to be a difficult task, and he soon lost interest. It was easier just to quit that place. His mother had not found out about the theft, and he gave a plausible excuse for leaving.

He got a new position, and things looked promising. He had not learned his lesson, however, for he stole a cap from his new employer. It may be granted that in each case there was strong provocation for his stealing. He wanted things which other boys had, and which he could not afford. The habit, however, of taking things was a dangerous one to form. He had got out of the first affair easily. If the habit were not to persist the second offense had to bring him some dissatisfaction. It was interesting to see the differing methods used by his mother and by the doctor to whom the affair had been reported. The first thing the latter did when he was told about it was not to blame the boy, but to talk it over with him on the basis of childish vs. mature reactions. At the same time the doctor assured the boy of his confidence in him. His mother's reaction was altogether different. As Donald said: "All she did was shame me and said she didn't see how I could come over here and face you, but she doesn't know you and how you talk."

The difference between the doctor and the boy's mother did not stop at this point, however. The latter seemed content to continue her attempt to shame him, hoping to arouse in him a deep sense of personal guilt. The doctor continued to express his confidence, but the screws came down when the question was raised of another position. The doctor insisted that Donald tell any prospective employer just why he had been discharged from his previous job, and no pleading could change him from this decision. He insisted that the boy face the full implications of what he had done; that was the only fair thing by an employer and the only way Donald would learn from his previous experience.

Even here he did not leave the boy isolated, for he offered to see personally anyone interested in employing Donald, explain the previous difficulties, and express his confidence in him. It was, none-the-less, a bitter pill the boy had to swallow as day after day he applied for positions only to be turned down when his record was given. When he did get a position, however, there was no further problem as regards stealing. He had learned his lesson.

Could it be said that the doctor punished him? Not in the sense of blaming him, or attempting to create any sense of guilt. That was what the doctor seemed most anxious to avoid. If, however, the definition of punishment which was given above is accepted, there was real punishment, even though the blame was omitted.

There seemed to be several reasons why this type of punishment was effective. In the first place Donald could not help realizing that in the usual sense no one had punished him; he had punished himself. His difficulty in getting another position, and all the humiliations involved, had not been imposed from without, but had been the inevitable result of what he had done. It was obviously fair that his new employer should know his record, but the experience of telling him was too painful to leave any desire for repetition. It followed that the punishment was of such a nature that its effectiveness was not lessened by feelings of resentment which might be directed at someone else. The punishment was not so much an *infliction* by somone else as it was an *affliction* which he had brought on himself.

There have been other illustrations of the effectiveness of punishment of this type where the one who received the punishment felt its justice and its inevitability; its justice because it appealed to him as being reasonable, its inevitability because it was the fruit of his own deeds. In three different cases, school children who proved intractable in the face of many kinds of punishment, including corporal, responded when they were demoted. They were told that since they could not behave as those of their age were accustomed to they would have to go with those who were younger, but they might return as soon as they had grown up. Here, too, the punishment grew out of their own acts; that was where the inevitability lay. There was no one trying to hurt them, and consequently no one to be resentful toward. None-the-less their antisocial behavior had brought unpleasant consequences which they were anxious to avoid in the future.

To refer again to the case of Donald Morio, the significance of the punishment lay in the fact that it was positive rather than negative. It suggested *future* alternative conduct, rather than *past* mistakes. There is much discussion at the present time as to the usefulness of feelings of guilt. Some consider them purely destructive, while others regard them as being inevitable if there is to be any reformation. Perhaps the issue might be more easily settled if it were recognized that at least the attitude should be prospective rather than retrospective. When the emphasis is on future conduct rather than past wrongs, the stress is on *learning* from the past, not on *blaming* oneself for it.

A correlative aspect of this forward-looking approach is that it consists of revealing unforeseen and disagreeable consequences, not of imposing unforeseeable penalties. Instead of there being fear or resentment, there is developed the habit of evaluation in the light of possible results.

It is sometimes felt that by this means wrongdoing would not be punished, but that the sinner would continue cheerily on his way. The exact opposite is the case. There might not be punishment in the sense of externally applied pain or injury; there would be genuine frustration. Paradoxically, this is often more unpleasant than a sharp and painful punishment which is administered by someone else. There was some end desired, the method of pursuit precluded its achievement, and furnished no other pleasures in its place. Obviously, the end and the method require examination and re-evaluation. The question of motives and responsibility will be dealt with later; suffice it to point out here that the method used with Donald required him to develop the habit of evaluating his conduct, of seeing the relationship of his act to future possibilities, and thereby developing the habit of responsibility.

It is also worth noting the way the doctor handled the question of social isolation; at one time letting Donald feel alone, and then seeing to it that he was very much a part of a group. At the same time that he was insisting that the boy face the situation in such a way as to make him inevitably feel lost, he was assuring him of his own friendship, and getting his family to assure him of theirs. There had to be enough isolation to make him realize that society disapproved of such an attitude toward the property of others, but that could not go so far as to cause a loss of confidence in himself, or make him concentrate upon finding some other group which would approve of his conduct.

The doctor did all he could to make sure that the boy's confidence in himself was not fundamentally shaken. When his mother shamed him, the doctor immediately tried to re-establish a friendly relationship, not denying that Donald had brought the situation upon himself, but stressing the more attractive future possibilities which he had the capacity to achieve.

Finally, the punishment was effective because it was recognized that there are limits to what punishment can do. The doctor saw the stealing as a *symptom* of a deeper problem; he set himself to deal with the underlying need, and not just with the symptom. The punishment could bring home a feeling of dissatisfaction with the habit of stealing. It could not cure the cause of the trouble, and it could not substitute new and better ways of acting.

In studying theories of punishment in the light of specific empirical data, it is necessary to refer again to Westermarck's attitude, bearing in mind the important fact that for him punishment was only incidentally for the purpose of control. Its primary function was to satisfy the emotional needs of the one punishing. He felt that a part of the instinctive equipment of man were emotions of resentment which, when aroused, demanded satisfaction. Punishment was the means of meeting this need, and was to be given with the express intention of inflicting pain. To be sure these emotions must not be allowed to run riot, but must be directed into channels of moral disapproval. In this way genuine moral control would result. None-the-less, punishment "first of all . . . wants to raise a protest against wrong."

If Westermarck's premise is true, that these emotions are instinctive and therefore largely inevitable in their expression, his position is plausible. The only thing one can do with resentment is to direct it into channels which have as many constructive, and as few destructive elements as possible. The final word at this point must be had by the psychologists. Three questions arise as regards the relationship of resentment or blame to moral control. Is it often a spontaneous reaction on the part of one who has been wronged? Is it an inevitable reaction? How adequate an instrument is it for control?

To the first question only one answer is possible; yes. That reaction is too nearly universal to be debatable. But is it inevitable? That is the real issue. Certain of the cases studied would seem to indicate that it is not as necessary a reaction as Westermarck assumed. There were a number of people observed whose strong initial resentment gave way to the desire to understand and control.

It is not implied that these feelings of resentment are immediately and easily dissipated when there is an attempt made to understand the causes lying back of the disliked behavior. Those emotional reactions are too deeply rooted to be easily displaced. There was, however, much evidence to indicate that slowly the habit of understanding might be built up, and that when that happened there was not the same outburst of resentment when an indignity was suffered. This is a partial answer to the question which is often put: "What outlet is there for feelings of indignation?" So long as there are such feelings, they will find expressions in resentment and blame, but are they necessary? Can they not over a period of time give place to a more objective desire for understanding.

Reference has already been made to Albert Hunt. His elder brother was continually enraged at him, and vented his wrath in numerous and severe beatings of Albert. During the course of treatment, this brother became interested in understanding Albert's problems, seeing in them a reflection of some of his own. The doctor explained the causes lying behind the behavior of each of them. The results may best be summed up in Albert's own words: "Raymond has been entirely different at home. He seems anxious now to help me. I guess we all understand things better." This incident was duplicated several times.

That understanding would lessen or remove anger, Westermarck does not doubt. He, himself, gave illustrations where this occurs, and gives the reason for it. It is because animals differ from men in that the motives of the former are understandable that: "we can hardly feel disposed to resent injuries which they inflict upon us." The fact seems to be that there was a fundamental premise, dogmatically asserted, that with human beings there cannot be an adequate understanding of the causes for wrongdoing. Wrong *must be* the result of deliberate perversity.

Such an attitude naturally throws the major stress on what types of punishment are most satisfying to the person whose feelings have been outraged, not on the types which will most adequately reform the wrongdoer. If this study has demonstrated anything, it is that punishment given under the stress of strong emotions of anger is ineffective and dangerous. It is not only apt to be capricious, but being born of resentment it results in the same feeling. The best that can be said of it is that it gives vent to emotions. Once again there emerges what seems to be one of the most persistent ethical problems to be faced: Is the attitude of blame consonant with control through a search for causes?

Our legal penalties, based almost universally on blame and guilt, with the consequent display of emotion, are open to the same criticism. There is need for a drastic revision of our penal codes and legal theories in the light of empirical data. Bentham, whose theories in many ways were an advance on those of his times, did not see that his program for "morals and legislation" was really a program for organizing conflict. His psychological data were so inadequate that he did not understand the way his punishment really worked. His theories were more adequate as a basis for class conflict than they were for achieving moral control.

Bain's attitude on blame is very different from that of Westermarck. He does not accept the assumption that wrong is a result of deliberate perversity. He sees it, rather, as the inevitable consequence of a given set of habits and motives. Under the circumstances there could have been no other outcome. Hence there is no attitude of blame, at least in the sense of making the individual feel he could have acted differently. Instead of blame there is a determination to furnish new incentives and motives which will produce different results another time.

There can be no doubt that such an attitude makes for effective social control. That is its goal. Consequently it is thoroughly empirical in character. Any means which will bring the desired results are good, and experiment and observation are the ways of discovering the right methods.

Certainly the punishment administered by those holding views such as Bain's would be very different from that studied in the first part of this chapter. It would not be given under the stress of anger, since there would be no more cause for anger in the case of what we call wrongdoing than there would be in illness. In fact it is illness which gives us the closest analogy to what Bain would have considered the condition of the wrongdoer. There would be an attempt to cure the patient, and the medicine would be that kind of punishment which would break down the old habits. It would not be aimed, however, at undermining the individual's confidence in himself, since there would be no implication that he could have acted differently. It would, however, introduce new factors so as to prevent a recurrence of the trouble. We do not want, at this point, to enter any metaphysical discussion of freedom and responsibility. Practically we can look for causes; we seem to find them. With that search comes understanding, and with that understanding comes a very different kind of control than that which is popularly practiced.

Any evaluation of Bradley would lead to similar conclusions to those reached with Westermarck. When there is a premise that "evil is done as evil and desired for its own sake" there is bound to be an attitude toward punishment different from that of Bain. As Bradley frankly admits, there is little concern with the social consequences of punishment. It was pointed out that he later modified his attitude toward punishment, but not his underlying theory. Certainly in his *Ethical Essays,* the primary objective is the creation of a sense of guilt, for guilt and blame are inescapable correlatives. The former is the product of the latter. Bradley explicitly affirms that if a man does wrong it is his fault.

He could have acted differently had he wished to, since even his wishes were not controlled by motives. Small wonder Bradley would want to arouse an acute feeling of guilt, of suffering, not primarily for the sake of reformation, but as a "denial of wrong" and an "assertion of right." It is this belief in perversity which creates the feeling of resentment, and it is this resentment which has proved so inadequate an instrument of control.

There is no point in minimizing the gulf which lies between two such writers as Bain and Bradley as regards their attitudes toward blame and guilt. There is a tendency at the present time to hold that there is no sharp distinction between them, that the feeling of dissatisfaction which Bain would arouse and the guilt which Bradley's blame would create are essentially the same. Each might be an instrument of social control. That is to miss the entire point, i.e., that guilt feelings and blame are not primarily for the purpose of control, but for the expression of resentment or "right." They are often positive hindrances to it. The cases studied furnished plenty of illustrations of this fact since it was the Bradley-Westermarck theory of punishment which, though not consciously, was the prevalent means of discipline.

The attitude of Donald Morio's mother was, of course, a case in point. When she discovered his stealing, her anger and humiliation found an outlet through the attempt to shame him, and make him feel his guilt.

Frank Holt, to whom reference has already been made, had never dreamed of an attitude which should not hold blame as a necessary result of "laziness" or "badness." Those words held all there was to say regarding such actions. There was nothing to understand as to possible causes, and this applied to his own faults as well as to those of others. Later, however, he became interested in the doctor's approach. The latter seemed always anxious to find the causes that lay back of actions and attitudes. One day Frank saw the implications of this approach, and in some astonishment remarked: "Now I see why you don't blame people for the things they do." The doctor had taught him to regard conduct problems, not as indications of meanness and perversity, but as symptoms of underlying difficulties. These symptoms would disappear only when the causes were found and dealt with. Blame and guilt were as irrelevant in the case of wrongdoing as they would be in illness.

There is, perhaps, an additional point to be noticed. It is not implied that no emotion is to be shown toward children, or adults either. It is maintained that control is made difficult by undisciplined emotions. A doctor *as doctor* must not show emotions; as parent he may. That is the anomalous and difficult situation in which parents find themselves. There must be an emotional relationship between their children and themselves, and yet when there is the problem of control the parents must take the attitude of the unemotional doctor. Because parents do not always see the necessity of this objectivity in control, the relationship between them and their children is often a mutual, emotional conflict. Nor can that situation be resolved until conscious control is divorced from unreflective emotion.

Why there has been this tendency to blame, and to arouse a feeling of guilt (which is Westermarck's problem), would take us into an historical and psychological analysis far beyond the bounds of this study. Unquestionably there have been genuine values at stake. It has given a certain kind of control; indeed it has seemed the only means of control possible. But it has been a control bought at a heavy price. It has taken the consequences into account too little, and the rough and ready instruments have often been futile and sometimes fatal.

The implications of a theory which stresses blame and guilt need to be made explicit. This attitude seems to make people either indifferent or actually hostile to the search for causes and cures. This point has been made many times, but it needs reiteration. The case of Mildred Kent is only one of many incidents which might be adduced. Her teacher said that she was "lazy, careless, impudent, and disobedient." The final straw came during a fire drill when the children were ordered to leave the room. Mildred would not leave, and smiled through the entire performance. Her teacher rebuked her sharply, and her parents punished her severely without any apparent results. To be sure, her grandmother said that she had come over to her house afterwards, and had cried bitterly. It was not until the doctor started looking for the cause of the trouble that it was discovered she had serious glandular trouble plus the psychological handicap of being unable to make up her mind. She confided in the doctor that she wanted to take part in the fire drill, but that she felt paralyzed. Glandular treatment, together with a régime composed more largely of affection than of punishment, wrought a complete cure. The causes had been found and dealt with, as they could never have been so long as it was felt that she was just "lazy, careless, impudent, and disobedient." Although this was true, such a diagnosis closed the door to any further investigation and cure.

This analysis is summarized in Dr. Dewey's words:

"Judgment in which the emphasis falls upon blame and approbation has more heat than light. It is more emotional than intellectual. It is guided by custom, personal convenience and resentment rather than by insight into causes and consequences."

It is impossible to leave a study of punishment without a realization of how very difficult it is to make it a useful instrument for education and control. If punishment is to be effective, whether in home or school or prison, it must be regarded as a skill, or perhaps better, as an art difficult to be learned.

An interesting suggestion has been made by a man who has had much experience with the usual means of dealing with criminals, that the functions of determining guilt and of assessing punishment should be separated since they require different abilities and skills. Punishment in particular is becoming too technical a problem for the ordinary jurist. The older method of making punishment fit the crime has, as Harry Elmer Barnes has pointed out, been supplanted by making the treatment fit the criminal. This has meant that physicians and psychiatrists must prescribe the steps to be taken in curing him. For punishment in the usual sense must give way to skilled diagnosis and psychological and medical care.

Obviously, not all cases of control need such elaborate attention. Parents do not ordinarily call in an expert in order to deal with each case of discipline. Even here, however, there is need for a sharp division between passing judgment on an act and determining the punishment for it. The first may include an emotional overtone, the latter must not if it is to be effective. The physician may have a feeling of revulsion as he diagnoses a loathsome disease, but he will do well to put that emotion behind him as he performs the operation. This may seem a counsel of perfection, and it is a goal difficult to attain. But if we are to be effective in rebuilding personalities, we must recognize the necessity of developing educational skills apart from emotions of blame and resentment. We must seek the causes lying behind behavior, and we must turn the eyes of parent and child, teacher and pupil, judge and criminal to past mistakes only to the extent that they throw light on future possibilities.

Chapter II

ENCOURAGEMENT, AFFECTION, AND
MORAL CONTROL

It is interesting to note how little attention has been given by ethical theorists to the positive side of moral education. Even among those who have felt keenly the need for control there has been far more interest in punishment than in encouragement or praise. Bentham's attitude has been the common one, i.e., that though praise might be effective it was much more difficult to administer than punishment, and that the latter instrument was therefore likely to be more effective. This assumption has been carried over into a general lack of interest in the conscious use of praise and encouragement.

Westermarck's attitude on this issue was similar to his belief as to the function of punishment. Praise is primarily for the satisfaction of the one who is praising, and only incidentally for the benefit of the one praised. The dangers of this type of praise are as obvious as they are with punishment similarly administered. It is uncritical and all too likely to fix bad rather than good habits. The one praising is apt to be so emotionally involved that he is unable adequately to evaluate the results.

Bain, with his clear insight into the place of satisfactions in the establishment of habits, devotes more time to the question of "rewards." He recognizes how large a place they have, and the need of supplying them, but the very word "reward" is an indication of his attitude. He seems to feel that rewards are something in the nature of a gift which, strictly speaking, is not deserved, but which is bestowed in order to make sure that the action approved is accompanied by some pleasant feeling, so that the individual may come to the place where he does not need these rewards. This is an attitude which needs empirical examination. What should be our attitude toward rewards and praise? Should we regard them as something over and above "justice" to be given as a generous recognition of right conduct, and therefore deserving of gratitude; or should they be considered in the light of natural and inevitable concomitants of certain courses of action?

The preceding chapter stressed the fact that punishment is necessarily negative, that its primary function is to help break down destructive habits, and pointed out that it can do little in the way of forming new patterns. If the last state of the man is not to be worse than the first, punishment must be followed by a definite attempt to build new habits on a more satisfying basis. Praise and the technique for encouragement deal with this more positive side of moral education and control. As an understanding of the causes of the trouble was seen to be essential to any intelligent punishment and any fundamental cure, so *an insight into the basic psychological needs is necessary to any effective encouragement and control.* For praise and encouragement are concerned with the strengthening of those tendencies which make for a happy, normal life.

Throughout the first section the close correlation between ethics and psychology has been apparent. Even in the theories of those men who have seemed to take little interest in psychology, and who have erected their ethical systems without regard for it, there has been implicit throughout, a definite psychological basis. This is not said in criticism. It is inevitable that it should be so, and the more explicit this basis becomes the more open will the ethical system be to examination and verification.

The ethical theorist must be concerned with the question of motives and springs of action. There have been theories enunciated which have blithely disregarded these issues, but, to the extent they have done so, they have done violence to human nature, and have proved themselves inadequate. This insight into basic motives is doubly important to any study of the development of moral responsibility, and for that reason it is necessary to recapitulate briefly the beliefs of certain of the men just studied before going on to formulate the psychology which has grown out of this study.

One of the virtues of Bentham was that he was explicit in his psychology. We may criticize its inadequacy, but at least we can see, and evaluate, the basis of his theory. For him the question of human motives was very simple. Men were moved solely by the desire for pleasure and the fear of pain. There was a continuous calculation for the purpose of achieving these ends. Human nature was essentially passive, awaiting the stimulus of pleasure or pain to arouse it to action. The question why anyone should recognize social obligations he answered by postulating a social instinct.

Bain accepted the pleasure-pain psychology with certain important modifications. Human nature, for him, was not passive but active, needing no stimuli to move it. For this reason the motives, i.e., the desire for pleasure and the fear of pain, were directional. Bain, also, made a large place for habits. The infant's first blind activities become crystalized into habits when they result in satisfaction, and these habits, themselves, become propulsive. Hence there is not a continual calculation of possible pleasures and pains. Finally, he did not postulate any distinctive social instinct. If a child grows up with social attitudes it is simply because he has found such behavior satisfying, and has formed habits of so reacting.

The primary motive for Bradley was self-realization. The difficulty comes in attempting to ask why there should be this goal. Pleasure, satisfaction, does not require a further "why"? It is its own justification. But it does seem legitimate to peer into the reason for trying to realize ourselves. At times, as was pointed out, Bradley implied that the ultimate reason is that such realization is satisfying, since there is the felt assertion of the will, than which nothing can be more pleasurable. He did not, however, consistently maintain this view, since that would seem to put us all on the common basis of seeking our own satisfaction, and this would remove any basis for responsibility. There might be mistakes; there could hardly be deliberate wrong. The basic motives for Bradley remained, therefore, essentially mysterious. His analysis, nevertheless, of the satisfactions involved in the felt assertion of the will is worth remembering.

It is interesting to observe wherein Dr. Dewey agrees with the preceding writers, and wherein he differs. He seems to be in complete agreement with Bentham's empiricism, but he definitely rejects his continuous pleasure-pain calculus. He is most emphatic in affirming, with Bain, the fact that life is essentially active rather than passive. He is also in agreement with Bain in making habit central. His sharpest disagreement would be with Bradley when the latter divides the personality into character and self, making the character subject to natural causes, but placing the self outside the stream of natural events. This belief breaks with Dr. Dewey's most fundamental faith, i.e., his thoroughgoing naturalism.

For him the personality, self, habits, whatever one may choose to call the essential core of human nature, is the product of purely natural forces, taking its rise in time, and having a definite, temporal history. Hence, though there may be aspects which are not as yet understood, there is nothing inherently mysterious about human beings.

This naturalism holds wide implications for any understanding of motives. Human beings are to be seen in the same light as all animal organisms. Just as the latter do not require "motives" for living, neither do human beings. Life is its own justification. It is true, however, that specific choices do have to be made, and motives become, then, judgments taking place in the stream of activity, giving direction to it. Involved in his position would seem to be the attitude that these motives must ultimately be equated with satisfactions, although he nowhere makes this explicit.

What seems inadequate in Dr. Dewey's psychology is that satisfaction has not been defined in sufficiently specific terms. The statement that living is its own end is insufficient. Satisfaction is concerned with *satisfying needs,* and, therefore, we must at least be definite as to what are the primary needs. These needs are not to be interpreted in rigid terms. They may be met in many ways, but any attempt at moral control which simply ignores them is bound to fail.

In discussing these needs it should be made clear that the

evidence for so regarding them rests on their success as techniques. That is, because certain ways have been found for making life healthy, we assume these methods are effective because they are meeting the wants of the organism. Certain techniques for control work; therefore, we conclude that they are meeting specific needs.

It would seem from this study that there are at least two such needs: achievement and affection. The former may be interpreted in many different ways, but it is bound up with what seems to be a fundamental desire to grow, and to accomplish. Just what this growth or accomplishment is to include will be determined largely by the group in which the individual finds himself. When this need, however, is not met in some form or other, there is trouble. The need for affection, also, has many outlets, from the infantile desire for care to the mature desire to feel that one is a part of a group, but the need persists. There are obviously other needs, physical and psychological, which must be met if life is to develop healthily and happily. These two, however, seem to be primary.

It was not easy to discover what fundamental problems lay at the root of Frank Morrisey's troubles. Partly by analysis of his difficulties, partly through experimentation, they were finally found and met. There was in the first place a very decided lack of confidence. For some reason there had been a growing sense of inferiority, and this had to be dealt with before there could be any genuine improvement. It seemed to center in a feeling that he was not the physical equal of other boys of his age. When he played, he wanted to be the boss, trying to demonstrate to others and to himself that he was a competent leader. When he came to the doctor his most important question was how to get strong, and he responded immediately to a recognition of developing strength. That was the doctor's first point of attack; he not only showed him how he could develop physically, but he continually praised him for each bit of advance.

Another means which was taken to help him have the sense of developing maturity was to interest him in being a good influence for his younger brother. That appeal called forth his latent capacities, and gave the doctor further opportunities for establishing his confidence. There seemed to be no need for punishment in this case even though he was unruly and disobedient. Instead of disciplining him, his parents and teachers were urged to look for opportunities to praise him. It struck his mother as a curious procedure to ignore his temper tantrums, and continually look for opportunities for praise, when the need for blame and punishment was so much more obvious.

The praise, of course, was not applied indiscriminately. It was simply the open recognition of his attempts to grow up. After he had achieved genuine maturity, and was convinced of it, there would be far less need of social recognition of the fact. While he was insecure it was necessary to strengthen every tentative move in the direction of maturity and achievement.

There was the same approach when it was found that he was not going to pass at school. The mother was seen at once and persuaded not to stress the fact of his failure, since that would only increase the inferiority which was at the root of his trouble. At the same time she was urged to explain to him how this would give him a better opportunity to lay a solid foundation for his future education. There was to be no punishment, but encouragement and stimulus only. He had no confidence in himself, and until it could be built up there was no hope of his forming constructive habits.

The case of Sidney Sharp was interesting as a clear illustration of the need for a feeling of achievement. Certainly he had had little enough of it. His mother admitted that she had not wanted him, and had probably shown it. The only attention he got from his father was a thorough and frequent beating. Small wonder if he did not think this was "the way to make me good," and that he had never developed any confidence. His problems began to be solved when he was given responsibility at home and at school, and, what is equally important, plenty of praise when he accepted it. Nothing could seem quite so wonderful to the boy as the fact that his family actually trusted him, and that "even Ruth has respect for me now."

Frank Holt had never been allowed to shift for himself. Each decision had been made for him. He got a job in an orchestra for the summer; his mother refused to let him take it. His first real adventure occurred when he worked in a store and earned enough to buy a suit of clothes. He wanted praise for this, and he got it in large quantities from the doctor. Having no self-reliance at all, he needed tremendous encouragement to continue to show some initiative. When he had gained confidence in himself and realized his capacities for growth and development, he no longer needed continual praise and encouragement, but it was some time before that point was reached.

Robert Rignana, thirteen years of age, had the most thrilling experience of his life when he was allowed to come the few blocks to the doctor's office by himself. He wanted to tell everyone about it, and he wanted everyone to tell him what an accomplishment it was. It represented to him a definite step in growth and achievement, and social recognition of it gave him the courage to take another step.

In many of the cases observed the parents expected thoroughly mature reactions from their children in certain realms of activity while discouraging it in others. Allen Hobart's mother said she had tried to encourage him, took him to the Park, gave him money when he wanted it, and still he continued to sulk and make trouble. Yet it was found that he had never been allowed to dress himself. The doctor showed him how to do so, and he responded at once to praise for his achievement. The same was true in school. Upon the advice of the doctor he was given special responsibilities such as passing out the papers, erasing the boards, and being monitor. His pleasure was apparent, but he needed recognition for whatever effort he put forth. Even so artificial a scheme as putting gold stars on a chart was tried with marked success. One was put on for each day during which his behavior had been good, and when he acquired seven in succession he was highly praised.

The case of Herbert Wells was very similar. When he was living with his mother, he was disobedient and quarrelsome, but when he was with his two aunts, he gave very little trouble. A hint as to the reason was given when it was discovered that his aunts gave him plenty of responsibility and praise for it, while his mother would not even permit him to dress himself. He would make an effort only when there was encouragement. His teacher complimented him in school one day for his penmanship. That was all that was needed to stimulate him to strenuous efforts to still greater perfection.

In each of the cases to which reference has been made, it is apparent that it was not merely indiscriminate praise which was of benefit. Praise unintelligently directed seems to be as dangerous as misapplied punishment. For praise, being nothing more than social recognition, can easily establish regressive habits. Praise can establish habits of stealing as well as of honesty, of quarrelsomeness as well as of courtesy. Without having recourse to some special social instinct, it certainly seems to be true that there is no more effective means of control than social recognition.

Rewards are powerful means of control, but like punishment or praise there must be discrimination between those which are effective and those which are ineffective. Our society is largely dominated by a belief that there must be extraneous rewards, financial or otherwise, if our actions are to be socially useful. The result is this concentrating of attention on what is going to be presented to us for our actions rather than whether our actions are of such a nature that they will intrinsically give us the sense of achievement, and thus meet that fundamental need. Giving a child a stick of candy may help to fix a right attitude, but how much more useful for the child to associate with right actions, not the candy, but a pleasurable sense of belonging to a group, and having social approval? The most basic praise or encouragement is not some artificial reward; it is recognition of a task well done which confirms an individual's own sense of achievement.

Even in this latter attitude there is an obvious danger which needs to be watched and studied. It is apparent that it would be possible to create an undue sense of dependence on social recognition, so that the individual would never learn to evaluate his own behavior. The cure for this, however, is not less social pressure, but care that part of the pressure is directed toward the development of independent persons who are capable of thinking for themselves. The point to be remembered is that this type of person is just as much the product of social pressure as are the most dependent people. As has been reiterated, there seems to be the need of a sense of achievement, but how achievement is to be defined will be determined by social environment. Our task is to see that included in it is the habit of independent evaluation.

The definition of what achievement is, will be determined by what gains social approval. If the group in which a child grows up gives praise and honor to the warrior, then this will largely determine the child's conception of what achievement is. If a parent tacitly or openly encourages habits of selfishness, those will be the attitudes which will be most apt to be fixed. Praise is a powerful instrument; it may also be a dangerous one.

We have been concerned so far in this chapter with the relation between praise and the sense of achievement. There is another need which is equally fundamental, and which has to be borne in mind in any positive approach to moral control. The child's (and adult's) need for affection may be an obvious one, but it seems to be easily forgotten.

Fear kept George Costello straight when he was at home. His father and mother were quick to punish on any provocation, and if they were not around at the right moment, his brother was only too ready to supply the deficiency. In fact, punishment and fear seemed to be about all that he did get out of his home. Neither punishment nor kindness worked at school, and he became more and more of a problem. Going on the assumption that at the root of any conduct problem was some unsatisfied need, the doctor looked over the general situation to see if he could find it. It was apparent at once that the boy was starved for affection. He received none at home, and only sporadic crumbs at school. The result was an attempt as persistent as it was unconscious to meet this need.

His own story as to the cause of his difficulties at school was very revealing. His present of the candy bell represented his attempt to gain the teacher's affection. He failed to see that his total conduct could hardly be glossed over by a piece of candy, and that it needed more than that if he were to be accepted. None-the-less, when the candy went on the shelf instead of being eaten, there was a real tragedy for George. The teacher had not eaten it, had not said "so nice" to him, and once more he was on the outside. It is equally understandable why he was excluded from the party. His previous conduct by no means justified his inclusion, and yet one can see what the incident did to him.

That the doctor's diagnosis was substantially correct is indicated by the change in attitude which followed after parents and teacher had been urged to give him more affection. There was improvement all along the line. In his case the responsibilities given him at school represented not so much an opportunity for a feeling of achievement as the assurance of being liked. It was significant that when he was with the principal, who had always liked him, he did not "have any behavior," and that he got A in conduct when there was a substitute teacher. His parents and his teacher persisted in ignoring his outbursts, and in showing him that he did "belong," that they were fond of him. The results justified the approach, and his problems at school were solved at the point when, with obvious delight, he could say: "I guess she likes me."

Ernest Conklin was ten years old when he was referred as being a problem both at home and at school. He had fits of temper, was disobedient, and fought steadily with other children. His father had died some years before, and the only other persons in his home were his mother and an older brother. These two, plus his teacher, were the important figures in his life. The most obvious aspect of the problem was Ernest's feeling, apparently justified, that his mother cared much more for his brother than she did for him. His brother was very critical of Ernest, and what attention he gave him was hardly of an affectionate kind. To his teacher, Ernest had been from the first a "problem," more apt to arouse annoyance than liking.

The doctor approached the case from the standpoint of these three people. His mother was shown what her partiality and lack of affection were doing to him. She had been largely unconscious of her attitude, and responded quickly. Ernest's brother was rather slower to see that he might be doing the boy harm, but he ultimately responded to the appeal to take the "big brother" attitude in a somewhat kindlier spirit. The teacher was the most helpful of all for she actively sought opportunities for making Ernest feel her interest and affection. He took pleasure in performing any little service for her such as sharpening her pencil or getting her books. It was only a short time until his school problems had cleared up, and the situation at home was indicated by his mother's comment to the doctor: "You sure were right when you told me better to be kind."

In Goodwin Carey's case the treatment was directed both

toward helping him to accept responsibilities which would give him a sense of achievement, and seeing that through affection he came to feel he was more a part of the family group.

It is not implied that any and all kinds of affection are equally valuable. It was quite apparent that there were certain kinds of love which weakened rather than strengthened; which so sheltered the child that there was little opportunity for a developing maturity. That was as fatal as no affection.

It may seem curious to suggest the necessity for *disciplined* affection, rather than that which is purely spontaneous. Perhaps, however, they are not entirely antithetical. Habits may be formed which will determine what kinds of affection are to be spontaneous. Certain it is that if an individual is to be developed fully there must not only be affection, but that of a kind which meets his fundamental needs.

There seems to be a close relationship between the two needs which have been discussed, i.e., for encouragement and for affection. They have to go together to be effective, for as affection seems almost dangerous apart from encouragement, so the latter seems ineffective apart from affection, and any theory of moral control must take these two needs into account.

CHAPTER III

THE ENVIRONMENT AND MORAL CONTROL

This chapter is concerned with the place of the environment in moral education. It is not possible to find sufficient evidence in the cases before us to explore fully this issue, but it is possible to examine the records with the view of determining to some degree the part the control of the environment played in the development of the children.

In trying to answer this question in the case of Walter King, one turns first to inquire what his environment was. Obviously the most important parts of it were the persons with whom he came into contact: his mother, father, sister, teachers, and the other children. It seems significant that, so far as we can determine, there was no change of attitude on the part of these people that did not provoke a reaction on his part.

The connection between Walter's problem and his father's difficulties was easy to see. There was continual friction between the two. Mr. King was very irritable, found it difficult to stand any noise or confusion, and punished violently on the slightest provocation. All of these attitudes, however, were simply symptoms of deeper difficulties. The home had been a pleasant one until the previous year, when Mr. King had injured himself. As a result, he lost his job, and had had difficulty both in finding, and in keeping, any position since that time. That had worried him until he had taken to drinking heavily. At each step in the descent his attitude toward Walter had become more critical. It was apparent that his illness was at the root of his difficulties, and, therefore, arrangements were made for him to have an operation. When he had recovered from that, he was helped to find a position. He stopped drinking, and with his major worries over it was possible for the doctor to enlist his cooperation in helping Walter.

The mother's problems were next dealt with. She was very resentful of the treatment she received where she was employed, and the difficulties preyed upon her mind. This problem was solved comparatively easily by a talk with her employer, and an explanation of Mrs. King's sensitiveness. One of the major difficulties with Walter's adjustment at school was his mother's avowed contempt for the teachers and their methods. It seemed impossible to do anything about this, and so the boy was finally removed from that school. With these annoyances off her mind, his mother was in a mood to respond more cordially to the suggestions made as to how Walter should be handled. She could see him more objectively.

It was not feasible to do much with the sister, though her destructive influence over Walter was quite apparent. She was, however, put in another grade so the two children would not be together, and this helped to solve Walter's problems even before he was sent to another school.

Because of Mrs. King's antagonism, it was impossible to adjust the boy completely. She changed her attitude somewhat, due to the suggestions from the doctor, and, in so far as she did so, there was a corresponding reaction on Walter's part.

It would seem to be the sheerest quibble to question whether what was done in this case was to control the boy through a manipulation of his environment, or whether there was just a removal of the obstacles which impeded his natural development. The fact remains that there seemed to be no control apart from a consideration of the environment in which he lived.

All of this, perhaps, seems obvious, almost as obvious as the ease with which it is forgotten. For as one studies the approach that was usually made by parents and teachers before the assistance of the doctor was sought, it becomes astonishingly apparent that it was just this factor of environment which was most frequently forgotten. It was rare for those in authority when they faced a problem, to examine objectively the physical and social environment, and thus determine the factors which were responsible for the child's behavior. It was much easier to blame, to punish. Though it would seem that the failure of this approach should have driven them to a search for objective causes, it rarely did so.

There was not a child studied who did not illustrate this problem of reconstructing the environment. At times it almost seemed that the patient was forgotten, as attention was directed toward solving the problems of those with whom he was associated.

A résumé of the various factors dealt with in the case of Harold Osgood seems almost amusing. Not only were there various approaches which specifically touched the boy, such as change of school, being sent to a summer camp, and instruction in music, but time and effort were spent in dealing with issues which would hardly seem to have a direct bearing. His father was treated for epilepsy; his mother was given a new set of teeth. And above all, the fear of poverty was removed.

In another case the child was largely ignored while the mother was dealt with. Arrangements were made for her to have an operation. She was worried about financial matters, and legal advice was provided. Finally, she was encouraged to go to night school so she could have more of a feeling of companionship with her children. In this way her child's problems were met.

In studying these cases to discover the relationship between moral control and environmental control it is illuminating to refer to the views of John Dewey and T. H. Green. Their sharp divergence throws light upon the issues with which we are concerned.

Central to any ethical system is the attitude toward the origin and development of the self, and it is to this issue that we must turn first.

For Dr. Dewey the self is thoroughly naturalistic. It is not a mystical entity introduced into the body at some stage of its development. There is no Platonic belief in the pre-existence of a soul. Rather the self is the natural product of a biological organism interacting with its environment. As this organism moves, lives, there is an inevitable interaction with that which is around it. The environment becomes part of it, and it is part of the environment, not "as coins are in a box, but as a plant is in the sunlight and soil." Out of this interplay develops, not only a body, but also a personality, a self. Obviously such a self, brought into being through natural forces is decidedly subject to causal sequences, and can only be controlled and modified through attention to causes.

Correlative to his attitude toward the environment is his belief that the self is a bundle of habits, and that "the problem of control . . . is the problem of habit, or more accurately, the problem of the environment in which habits are incorporated."

For Green, though the self has a naturalistic basis, it is not the result of purely naturalistic forces. As he puts it, there is an animal organism, which has its history in time, and which gradually becomes the vehicle of an eternal consciousness. And then, and not until then, is there in any genuine sense a personality or self. With such a premise it is inevitable that the self should not be regarded as a part of the natural order: "the agent is not a natural agent." Hence the self is only partially subject to natural causes. It is apparent what wide differences there are bound to be in the ethical systems of two men who differ so sharply in their fundamental psychological assumptions.

This difference carries over into their respective definitions as to what are morals. For Dr. Dewey "morals mean customs, folkways, established collective habits." They are the ways of reacting to the environment which have been found so satisfying that they have been passed on to later generations. There is nothing esoteric about them, nor is there a separate realm which may be labeled moral to the exclusion of some other. Whatever activities make for the good life come within the scope of morality. Here, again, it is apparent that there can be no possible consideration even of what constitutes morals apart from a consideration of what makes up the environment. *Morals are functions of the environment.*

For Green, no such definition is possible. Morals are not

the product of interaction of the organism with its environment; they represent, rather, the realization in this organism of the eternal consciousness bringing to actualization absolute, moral laws. These absolute laws cannot have a temporal history any more than the eternal consciousness can be in time. Whether or not these moral codes help in adjusting the individual to his environment, personal or physical, is irrelevant, althought it might be assumed that the eternal consciousness would so order things.

There is both agreement and divergence between them as regards the particular individual's relationship to the existing code. Dr. Dewey points out that an individual acquires the morality as he inherits the speech of his social group. Green could hardly deny so obvious a fact, nor is he disposed to do so. Their difference comes with regard to what the individual does with his inheritance. According to Dr. Dewey, he either blindly accepts it without much concern as to whether it serves its purpose, i.e., adjusts himself to his environment, or else he empirically evaluates it. In the light of his own personal experience, how satisfying is it? His fathers have said that it is wrong to lie. Why? May there not be times, even taking the long, rather than the short, view into account, when a lie helps? Dr. Dewey would hope that he had been so well educated that he would realize the social implications of his decision, but none-the-less that decision must ultimately be his own, tested by his personal experience.

Since, for Green, morals were not originally based on the attempt of the organism to get on in his world, but antedated both his own, and the racial, experience, there could be no basis for the individual's empirical examination of the social code; at least not from the standpoint of the satisfaction it gives. There is room for a close scrutiny to determine how fully it expresses the will of the eternal consciousness. The satisfaction involved is incidental to the determination to be an adequate vehicle for this eternal mind. It is through reason and the dialectical process that we discover the laws of morality.

The differences between the two men come to a natural climax over the question of what constitutes moral control. For Dr. Dewey, moral control and environmental control are inseparable. The self has come into existence through an interplay with the environment, and there is a causal relationship between them. Habits have been built up as responses to the world, and any change in the surroundings brings its inevitable change in character. He says: "A psychology based on habit will fix its attention upon the objective conditions in which habits are formed." In no other way can old habits be changed and new ones established.

Green cannot accept this conclusion because he disagrees with its main premise. The self does start out on a naturalistic basis; it has its beginning in an animal organism, but once it becomes a vehicle for the eternal consciousness, it is, to that extent, outside the chain of cause and effect. The problem lies in helping the individual achieve his goal of being a perfect vehicle. Here there is a place for a kind of negative environmental influence. It is possible for obstacles to be in the way of the realization of the ideal, and to the extent that we remove them we give the individual an opportunity he could not otherwise have had. Of course this removing of obstacles might be so interpreted as to make it mean the creation of ideal situations, in which case Green's position would differ little from that of Dr. Dewey. But though in practice they might be reconciled, in theory they are opposites, for Green cannot admit that controlling the environment is moral, since for him moral control is essentially internal control.

The question may be raised as to whether Green, as opposed to Dr. Dewey, was not standing for self-control. This would hardly be, however, an adequate statement of their differences. Both men would advocate self-control as the finest expression of character, but Dr. Dewey would insist that self-control is as much a product of natural causes as is lack of control, and that it is necessary to manipulate the environment so as to achieve this end.

For him, *self-control is social control,* since the former is the product of the latter. Social control becomes self-control at that point where society creates in the individual the capacity to evaluate and manipulate his own environment. The important point, however, is that whether the control is external or internal, it is still to be achieved through a change of environmental factors. The self is what it is as a result of purely natural forces; it must be changed by modifying the situation which determined its development. Self-control implies the habit of intelligent self-diagnosis, but the cure involves the ability to change the external factors. *Self-control is still environmental control.* It is hardly necessary to make more explicit the fact that this naturalism gives a genuine basis for control. In such a system, when an individual does not show the desired trait, it is possible to search for the cause of the difficulty, and then create an environment which will give the hoped-for result. This is as true for the individual who wishes to change his own habits as it is for the society which desires to educate a child or reform a criminal. In no case can there be success save as the environment which has created the situation is transformed.

Attitudes are formed through the interaction of the individual with society. Our morals are social because we have precisely the same relationship to society that a plant has to the earth. Society is the soil in which we grow, and to change the soil is to modify the plant. From the standpoint of control, this is a hopeful fact since it gives us a tangible means of directing the individual's development. In a non-naturalistic system the problem of moral control is a problem of "will" and hence of lifting oneself by one's bootstraps. The discoverable reasons why certain attitudes were developed, and therefore, the ways of changing them, are regarded as beneath moral contempt. *If moral problems are not conceived as social problems, we face an essentially sterile theory of ethics,* which must sooner or later dismiss even the problems of "self-control."

As one tries to discover why Green took the attitude he did, it becomes apparent that there was a consistent view running through his entire position. He was in the stream of Kant, opposing empiricism and especially naturalism. His strongest conviction was that morality is a term characterizing the conduct of only those persons who determine their own attitudes. Morals are internal in the sense that they are not ultimately social. This was in line with his epistemology, for he challenged the Empiricists to show how a series of sensations could know itself. He felt there must be a permanent, active self. Hence an idea cannot come from without into the mind; it must be the expression of the mind's own activity.

It is obvious that this attitude would have wide implications in the field of ethical theory. An object is pleasant only when a person considers it so. Pleasure and pain are not qualities of objects which are independent of the mind, and, therefore, the environment is not irresistible. What is external cannot affect choice just because it is external. It follows that the moral life is one of self-determination; that control is internal to the self. It is probable that Green was reacting from the very sharp contrast which Bentham had made between society and the individual, and from the largely external control which the utilitarians had advocated. In this reaction, however, Green created an ideal self which was independent of the external world.

This position involved the old controversy as to the relationship of the will to the desires. The idealists had to assume a separate faculty which could control the desires. If they were not, however, to find themselves in what was essentially the utilitarian position they had to keep this will out of the natural order. It must not be determined by its environment. It was that which made control so essentially mysterious a process. There was no way of educating or directing this will. The idealists, unwilling to become naturalists, yet desiring an objective will, attempted to gain a kind of control by identifying this internal will with the real will, which was society. We find, as a result, the attitude taken, especially by Bradley and Bosanquet, that the individual must participate in the will of society, must "will" the objective order.

Dr. Dewey's naturalism makes such a will superfluous, or rather he identifies it with our habits and institutions. These habits, having been developed under particular conditions, are susceptible to any change in the external situation, and hence there is no moral problem distinct from the problem of social control.

This discussion of the views of Green and Dr. Dewey has been necessary to prove that it is idle in practice to separate environmental from moral control. Certainly the cases studied substantiate this. When the environment could be modified, the child's attitude was changed. Most impressive of all were the cases in which the children were put in such a physical and social atmosphere that they learned to evaluate for themselves the effect of their own environment, and thereby to control themselves.

It cannot be urged too strongly that this issue is not one of internal vs. external control. The contention is rather that the only way we can develop a genuine inner self-control is through a consideration of the external factors. Is control possible apart from an adjustment of the conditions which created the situation? Nor is this a merely academic problem. Throughout our social and political fabric we are attempting to develop finer personalities, but with little regard for the external world in which people live. Men become criminals under specific conditions. We "punish" them, and then send them forth to the same environment which caused the trouble in the first place. We are engaged in a tremendous enterprise of child training, yet all too often we forget that the most powerful schoolmaster of all is the atmosphere, social and physical, in which the children are growing up.

Even among educated, intelligent people there is apt to be a strong reaction against the attitude that the causes for difficulties are to be found in the environment, that to the extent there are difficulties, they are symptoms pointing to an unsatisfying environment. To say that morals are functions of the environment seems to many people to throw over human responsibility.

The question of freedom and responsibility will be dealt with in the last chapter, but it is, perhaps, not pointless to refer here to this common reluctance to see human activity in naturalistic terms as the interplay of organism with its environment. One may in reply point out that it is just this discovery that the human organism is a product of natural forces which enables us to develop responsibility, since it keeps the personality in that world over which we are gradually gaining mastery. If it removes transcendental freedom, it substitutes responsible control.

There was one mother among the cases studied who suddenly realized the implications for her of this method of treatment. Andrew Cope was referred by his teacher as a behavior problem who was giving much trouble. An investigation revealed that his father had died, and that his mother was making him the repository of her sorrows and emotions. The doctor discussed the boy's problems with this fact in mind until Mrs. Cope pertinently remarked: "I see, it is not the children, it is the mother that needs to be investigated." She was right as far as she went. She had to be brought, however, to realize that she, too, was a product of her environment, and as such no more subject to blame than were her children; that only as she considered her environment could she control her own problems and those of her children.

Chapter IV

INTELLIGENCE AND RESPONSIBILITY

We have seen that the question of education and the development of responsibility cannot be discussed without reference to the problem of determinism. In fact, that may be said to be the central issue. Harry Elmer Barnes in *The Story of Punishment* says: "The greatest obstacle to successful education . . . resides in the popular theologico-metaphysical conception of man as a free moral agent, capable of arbitrary self-determination of conduct irrespective of physical ancestry or social experience. . . The chief opposition to scientific criminology arises from its fundamental and inevitable espousal of the psychological conception of determinism in conduct." Is Dr. Barnes right in maintaining that it is impossible to have education and control without a frank acceptance of the determinist position?

The question has usually been discussed from some metaphysical standpoint. Is the nature of reality such that causality is universal? While this battle raged, the values at stake were lost sight of, and it has been this fact which has made the controversy impossible of solution. A careful examination might indicate that the values which it was thought could only be maintained by indeterminism actually are lost unless there is a complete determinism.

It should be pointed out that determinism and mechanism are not necessarily identical. The latter seems to reduce human personality to the level of a machine, and there has been a natural reaction against such a position. There is, however, a determinism which, because it implies intelligence, seems actually to make human freedom possible. The issue, then, is this: is determinism rather than indeterminism the basis of moral responsibility?

Certainly one of the major values involved in the controversy over determinism is that of responsibility, and it is necessary to recognize that there are two approaches to this question.

On the one hand are those who are primarily concerned with an evaluation of past behavior. For them responsibility is an a priori fact to be accepted as a basis for assessing praise or blame. That is not, however, what is involved for those who are primarily interested in education. Responsibility for them is not an inward look, involving a metaphysical and mysterious issue of freedom. They assume that responsibility is a habit which must be developed precisely as any other habit. The past is significant for the light it may throw on causes, since only in that way is control to be found. This fact cannot be overstressed; responsibility has a very different definition according to whether we are looking to the past or to the future. In the former case, it is a *feeling* or intuition. When our eyes are turned to the future, responsibility becomes a *possibility,* a *habit* of meeting life in such a way that growth takes place and there is an acceptance of responsibilities.

Bradley is an excellent illustration of one who takes the former attitude toward responsibility. His *Ethical Studies* are primarily concerned with this issue, and it becomes the norm by which he builds his entire ethical system.

He starts his discussion by a disavowal of freedom, as it is commonly understood, as involving, not responsibility but chance. He sees clearly the implications of the indeterminist position; that when the self is separated from the sequences of cause and effect, there is no hope for education or control. The result is "a wholly unaccountable creature."

He is, however, as emphatic in rejecting determinism. There is the belief that this view will, even more surely, remove any possibility of responsibility. His argument is that we *feel* free, and "never for one moment doubt that we are responsible." He, thus, sees two sides to the argument, and apparently has no love for either. The solution which he ultimately reaches has already been referred to, and we have seen that it practically amounts to an acceptance of the indeterminist viewpoint, in spite of the objections which he has marshalled against it. He removes the self from the naturalistic realm of causes, making it essentially mysterious both as to origin and control. He is quite explicit in recognizing that this precludes any understanding of the self or will.

There must have been deep values which he was trying to preserve, or he would not have taken a position where he was obviously not entirely at home. They seem to lie in his definition of responsibility. He felt the necessity of being able to look back over a course of action, and assess praise and blame. Responsibility could only be preserved by removing the self from the natural world.

In taking this view, he was holding a belief which has had almost universal acceptance. What is the meaning of responsibility if it does not involve this ability to pass judgment on persons? There has hardly been an ethical system, to say nothing of a religion, which has not had this attitude at its heart.

In contrast with this view is the position of those who are less interested in *assessing* responsibility for what *has* been done than in *developing* it for the sake of what *is* to be done, who are more interested in the future than in the past. To one interested in control rather than in blame the *all-important question is not whether a person is responsible but whether he accepts responsibilities.* That issue can be discussed without any reference whatever to the old free-will-determinism controversy. The crucial problem is whether or not we can develop this habit of responsibility, and it is this which is subject to empirical examination. There are two questions to be answered. Is there in the organism a potential capacity which can, under proper environmental conditions, be developed into the habit of responsibility? If that seems to be the case, what are these conditions?

In studying the case of Frank Holt, it is apparent that there were ambivalent tendencies at work. The old habits which did not involve the acceptance of responsibilities had given satisfaction but there was a decided feeling of frustration, of being blocked as he tried to reach out to a more mature way of life. He liked to have his parents supply his wants, but he wished to say what those wants should be. His parents were dubious about his capacity for accepting responsibility since they had seen so little indication of it. When Frank, however, realized that if he were to meet the desires which arose with developing maturity, he would have to take the responsibilities that went with them, he showed a surprising ability to accept them. In a real sense he developed that capacity because he realized that unless he did so he could not have the things, the satisfactions, which he wanted. He was willing and able to mature, and accept the growing responsibilities, when he found that the satisfactions on the new level were greater than those he could have on the old. That would seem to be the first condition for the development of this habit of responsibility.

There was an interesting illustration of the principle that growth has to be associated with satisfactions found in the case of Malcolm Barnes. Although he was nearing five years of age, he was showing marked reluctance to dress, feed himself, or, indeed, to accept any responsibilities. The doctor suggested to his mother that she encourage him by saying that these were the things that every boy did when he grew up. Malcolm promptly retorted that he did not want to grow up, and the problem did not seem to be any nearer solution than it had been before. A study was made to see why he reacted this way, and it was found that he had come to associate growth with largely unsatisfying experiences. His mother was urged to cease mentioning the word for a time except in connection with highly pleasurable experiences. For the next few weeks whenever he had a thoroughly good time someone would casually remark that it was because he was growing up. It was a matter of only a few weeks until he made the transfer, and growth became associated with satisfactions. At that point he responded to the appeal to grow up as regards eating and dressing. In fact, he became something of a nuisance in his demands for further opportunities to demonstrate his sudden maturity.

Herbert Wells was an illustration of a child who was making strenuous attempts to break with his infantile reactions, and take on more mature ways, with all that implied.

It was his mother who blocked him at every turn. She was divorced from her husband, and centered her entire emotional life upon her one child. When it was suggested that he would have a splendid opportunity for development in a summer camp, her reply was: "What do you mean; me to be without Herbert? What on earth would I do without him? What could I do nights?" His aunts were very different. They treated him as a responsible boy. His mother could not understand why his behavior was so much better when he was with them than when he was at home. She did not see any connection between his infantile behavior and her insistence that, though he was eight years of age, she should continue to dress him. Herbert had apparently realized through his contacts with other boys that, on the whole, maturity with its responsibilities was more satisfying than remaining an infant. When Mrs. Wells was given other outlets for her emotional life, there was little difficulty in her way of encouraging Herbert to grow up.

We have spoken of the place of satisfaction in developing the habit of responsibility. It may be well to refer to some of the conclusions reached previously, and point out that praise and blame for meeting, or failing to meet, our expectations are not as desirable as simply *holding* a person responsible, i.e., by allowing him to feel the consequences of his responsibility or irresponsibility.

One has only to state the problem of responsibility to answer it. The above cases have illustrated, what we all know, that it is possible to form the habit of responsibility, and that it must be formed as any habit is developed, through making it satisfying to actual needs. Psychological insight plus a practical skill in manipulating the environmental factors produces the habit of responsibility. The point needs to be stressed that in this development of responsibility, indeterminism would be a fatal barrier because there could be no dependence on the individual's response to education.

Throughout this discussion there has been the implicit recognition that responsibility is something more than a blind, mechanical response to physical causes. Inherent in any genuine responsibility is intelligent foresight of consequences. This raises the problem which was referred to at the beginning of the chapter. Is it possible to reconcile intelligence with determinism? This question cannot be answered without a brief analysis of what we mean by intelligence.

It should be made clear that this term is used in the descriptive sense and not with the technical meaning given it in recent years by certain schools of psychology. It is used to describe that process which has to do with the effective use of one's capacities. Hence it is used in much the same sense as the word "understanding."

The explanation which would seem to be most in line with the facts observed implies an acceptance of a naturalistic or biological viewpoint. An organism interacting with its environment develops certain patterns or habits, ways of handling its situation. At a certain stage these habits begin to impede each other, not being altogether unified in their demands. The self is confronted by conflicting ends. At this point another habit is developed, i.e., the habit of intelligence or foresight. This habit, being a product of the natural world, is as much determined as is any other response.

The function of intelligence is to evaluate the competing objects or motives by seeing them in larger perspectives. The degree to which this habit of evaluation has been developed will determine the extent to which an individual can withhold action until the most permanently satisfying conduct is recognized. Such a decision liberates the self to move securely and continuously in the direction of its choice.

Intelligence is not the expression of some mystical self standing apart from the natural world, nor the coercion of a part of the self by another part. It is a capacity for evaluation. It is the recognition that certain ways of action are more in line with the total character than are some others, and, with this realization, a choice of that course which will in the long run give the greatest satisfaction. It is a refusal to permit an immediate emotion to dominate a reluctant self.

Intelligence, then, is that capacity of the self which guarantees that mechanical causality will not be the only kind of causality. *Because* intelligence is determined, is subject to a chain of cause and effect, it is possible for it to be developed to that point where it gives the promise that a human being may grow along consistent lines which are predictable and consciously aimed at. Freedom is not an inheritance; it is an achievement. The free man is the intelligent one. To quote again a sentence of Dr. Dewey's: "The road to freedom may be found in that knowledge of facts which enables us to employ them in connection with desires and aims." *Freedom is intelligent choice* between available possibilities, *not undetermined choice.*

Indeterminism does not mean that the genuine needs will find their satisfaction. It means that chance or blind mechanism must control. Psychological determinism implies that to the extent that there is intelligence, those motives will be followed which give expression most fully to the total self.

To the extent that there is this determinism, will there be freedom of the self to realize its highest aims. Motives without intelligence means mechanism; motives with intelligence means freedom. It is intelligence determined by its motives which *saves* personality. We value freedom too deeply to want indeterminism; we value personality too highly to want to see it the pawn of mechanism.

To redefine determinism from another angle, it is simply the past in interplay with the present. A determined self is an empirical self. It should be made clear, however, that the process of making a choice is really a process of making a new preference. It is not simply the old desire; it is the old plus the new, and in that situation a new self is produced. This needs to be emphasized. The self is not a mere effect of antecedent causes, for the reason that it is creatively remaking itself in the light of its developing experience.

Dr. Dewey's analysis of thinking is in line with this view. He considers it the imaginative rehearsal of various possibilities until one of them is seen to be more in line with the preferences of the organized body of habits. Thinking is evaluating all motives until the most satisfying one has a chance to come into play. In that sense *the habit of intelligence is the habit of responsibility.*

We have, therefore, to examine this habit of responsibility from a somewhat different angle. Is it possible to develop a habit of evaluating various possibilities? Here, again, to state the problem is to answer it. We know we can develop this attitude of deliberation, although all-too-little attention is given to doing so. The case of Edward Perry is relevant because it tells the story of a boy who did develop the habit of consciously choosing his goal, and therefore became responsible. Edward's difficulties were solved largely through an appeal to his ability to evaluate consciously his behavior. He had been dominated by immediate emotions, he had not taken the long view. When the various courses of action were pointed out to him, he saw that he was not choosing in such a way as to give him the most fundamental satisfaction. With that realization came the beginning of the desire to mature, and to accept the responsibilities which were implicit.

We have stressed the place of intelligence in moral control, and the fact that it can function only to the extent that it sees the competing motives and understands the underlying forces which are in operation. The case of Albert Hunt furnishes an interesting illustration of the deep influence which such understanding has.

Albert found his problems unsolvable so long as they were mysterious. When he could not see the motives at work, both in his own behavior and in his brother's, there was resentment and an inability to cope with the situation. As soon, however, as he saw the forces that were in operation he was able to handle them. This understanding was, of course, too new to function completely, and there was no final solution until both he and his brother saw what was involved. There was the same sense of surprise on the part of each when they suddenly realized the causes which had lain back of their attitudes.

The most obvious result was the tolerance which each came to have toward the other. Their resentment gave way to a desire for understanding, when they realized that neither had been perverse. They saw that, under the given circumstances, no other behavior had been possible. The proverb: "To know all is to forgive all," is frequently quoted as being the ultimate expression of tolerance. But where there is genuine understanding, a more adequate statement would be: "To know all is to remove any need for pardoning."

Not only did understanding bring tolerance to these two boys, it also gave them control over their own actions. With a realization of their own motives, and a clearer insight into their genuine desires, they were able to choose deliberately the direction in which they wished to move. Their problems were solved when Albert could say: "I guess we all understand things better."

It is apparent, then, that the problem of the development of responsibility eventuates, in the final analysis, in a search for means to develop intelligence. Moral education is thus not merely external control. It is rather the development of a series of responses by the individual to meet the requirements of a course of action in which he is engaged. Its consequences have a sufficiently purposive hold to keep him persisting toward the end. The distinctly moral in what he does is living up to the highest possibilities of the particular activities in which he is engaged.

The word "education" has at times in this study been used interchangeably with "control." It is recognized that there are many types of control, physical, coercive, legal. The kind of control in which we are interested, however, is a form of education, a skill in developing intelligence. No question in education is more persistent than the old Socratic query: "Can virtue be taught?" From our standpoint the answer is "No! but intelligence may be developed, and that is the essence of virtue, as it is of responsibility."

Nor does intelligence imply simply seeing consequences; it means also *feeling* them. As Dr. Dewey has pointed out, thought and emotion cannot be separated. "To put ourselves in the place of another ... is the surest way to attain universality and objectivity of moral knowledge." Without this capacity for imaginatively living through experiences that affect both ourselves and others there is no possibility of creating a sense of responsibility, and no intelligence which lacks this capacity deserves the name. It was this realization which led Shelley to say that "the great instrument for moral good is the imagination."

Intelligence has often been contrasted with imagination, but if our analysis is correct, they are not antithetical, but two aspects of a single process. The ability to enter imaginatively the experience of others, to foresee possible consequences for them, is what is meant by the term "sympathy." Intelligence, imagination, sympathy, they are all aspects of a capacity for moral knowledge.

The specific ends of education have not been defined in other than general terms. It has seemed that the question of control might be discussed apart from the problem of value. We have used for purposes of illustration whatever goals people have actually adopted. After all, the question here is not universal moral legislation, but insight into particular techniques. The problem of moral ends, and the basis on which they are chosen, is, in its final analysis, a matter of taste.

There is not room for an adequate discussion of this view other than to say that it has inevitably grown out of the conclusion that there is no absolute moral code which may be intuitively reached. Morals must be regarded as skills, arts, ways of handling the environment, and the ultimate norms are satisfactions and enjoyments. Such conclusions point to an ethical code where each separate situation is unique, to be dealt with in the spirit of the artist.

BIBLIOGRAPHY

BAIN, ALEXANDER. The Emotions and Will, 3d ed., Appleton, 1888.

BARKER, ERNEST. Political Thought; from Herbert Spencer to the Present Day, Holt, 1915.

BARNES, HARRY E. The Story of Punishment, Stratford, 1930.

BENTHAM, JEREMY. An Introduction to the Principles of Morals and Legislation, 2d ed., Oxford, 1879.

────── The Rationale of Punishment. Tait, Edinburgh, 1843.

BERNARD, L. L. Instinct, Holt, 1924.

BLATZ, W. E. and HELEN BOTT. The Management of Young Children, William Morrow & Co., 1930.

BRADLEY, F. H. Ethical Studies, G. E. Stechert, 2d reprint, 1927.

────── Some Remarks on Punishment, *International Journal of Ethics*, IV, 269.

BURNHAM, W. H. The Normal Mind, Appleton, 1924.

CAMERON, H. C. The Nervous Child, Oxford Medical Publications, 1919.

CHILDS, JOHN L. Education and the Philosophy of Experimentalism, Century, 1931.

COE, G. A. The Motives of Men, Scribners, 1928.

CONSTANCE, E. E. Rational Hedonism, *International Journal of Ethics*, V, 79.

DAVIDSON, W. L. Political Thought: the Utilitarians, Holt, 1916.

DEWEY, JOHN. Democracy and Education, Macmillan, 1916.

────── Experience and Nature, Open Court, 1925.

────── How We Think, Heath, 1910.

────── Human Nature and Conduct, Holt, 1922.

────── The Quest for Certainty, Minton, Balch, 1929.

Dewey, John. Reconstruction in Philosophy, Holt, 1920.

Dewey, John, and J. H. Tufts, Ethics, Holt, 1908.

Ewing, A. C. The Morality of Punishment, Kegan Paul, Trench, Trubner & Co., 1929.

Fite, Warner. Moral Philosophy, Lincoln MacVeagh, 1925.

Green, T. H. Principles of Political Obligation, Longmans, 1890.

––––––– Prolegomena to Ethics, Oxford, 1883.

Harris, P. E. Changing Conceptions of School Discipline, Macmillan, 1928.

Hobhouse, L. T. The Rational Good, Holt, 1921.

Hurlock, Elizabeth. The Value of Praise and Reproof as Incentives for Children, "Archives of Psychology," no. 71, 1924.

James, William. Principles of Psychology, Holt, 1892.

––––––– The Dilemma of Determinism. (In The Will To Believe, Holt, 1897).

Kilpatrick, W. H. Foundations of Method, Macmillan, 1925.

Laski, Harold J. The Dangers of Obedience, Harpers, 1930.

Lineham, J. Sin and Sacrifice, *International Journal of Ethics*, XVI, 88.

Lund, F. H. Emotions of Men, McGraw-Hill, 1930.

McDougall, William. An Introduction to Social Psychology, Luce, 14th ed., 1921.

––––––– Outline of Abnormal Psychology, Scribners, 1926.

Meyer, Adolf. Freedom and Discipline, *Progressive Education*, V, 3.

Mill, J. S. Utilitarianism, "Everyman's Library," Dutton, 1910.

Miller, Marion. Rewards and Punishments, "Studies in Child Training," Ser. I, no. 2, Child Study Association.

Moore, G. E. Principia Ethica, Macmillan, 1903.

Otto, M. C. Things and Ideals, Holt, 1924.

Otto, M. C. and F. C. Sharp. A Study of the Popular Attitude Toward Retributive Punishment, *International Journal of Ethics*, XX, 341.

PALMER, G. H. The Problem of Freedom, Houghton, 1911.

RASHDALL, HASTINGS. The Theory of Punishment, *International Journal of Ethics*, II, 20.

—— The Ethics of Forgiveness, *International Journal of Ethics*, X, 193.

ROGERS, A. K. English and American Philosophy since 1800, Macmillan, 1922.

—— Morals in Review, Macmillan, 1927.

RUSSELL, BERTRAND. Education and the Good Life, Boni & Liveright, 1926.

SETH, JAMES. The Theory of Punishment, *International Journal of Ethics*, II, 232.

SHARP, F. C. Ethics, Century, 1928.

SIDGWICK, HENRY. The Methods of Ethics, Macmillan, 6th ed., 1901.

STAPLEDON, W. O. A Modern Theory of Ethics, Methuen, 1929.

STEPHEN, LESLIE. English Utilitarians, Putnam, 1902.

TAYLOR, A. E. Self-Realization—a Criticism, *International Journal of Ethics*, VI, 356.

THOM, D. A. Everyday Problems of the Everyday Child, Appleton, 1928.

THOMSON, M. K. The Springs of Human Action, Appleton, 1927.

TROLAND, L. T. The Fundamentals of Human Motivation, Van Nostrand, 1928.

WARDEN, C. J. Animal Motivation Studies, Columbia Univ. Press, 1931.

WESTERMARCK, E. A. Origin and Development of the Moral Ideas, Macmillan, 1908.

WILSON, MARGARET. The Crime of Punishment, Jonathan Cape, 1931.

WOODWORTH, R. S. Psychology, Holt, 1921.

—— Contemporary Schools of Psychology, Ronald Press, 1931.

ZACHRY, C. B. Personality Adjustments of School Children, Scribners, 1929.

INDEX

VITA

Laurence Milton Sears was born in Oneida, New York, April 10, 1896. He graduated from the Gloversville High School in 1914, and received his A.B. from Princeton University in 1918. He attended Union Theological Seminary, 1920-23, and devoted his time to graduate work in Columbia University in 1928. During the session 1929-30 he was instructor in Seth Low Junior College, Columbia University. In the fall of 1930 he was appointed assistant Professor of Philosophy at Ohio Wesleyan University, Delaware, Ohio, where he is at present Associate Professor and Acting Head of the Department of Philosophy.